Invitation to discovery

Bruges

Franck Ferrand

Photographs by Christian Sarramon

lannoo

supermarkt

CONTENTS

CHARM AND ENCHANTMENT

CHARM AND ENCHANTMENT

There, there is nothing else but grace and measure,
Richness, quietness, and pleasure
CHARLES BAUDELAIRE
Invitation to the Voyage

Many people come to Bruges to see for themselves the sights that they know from books and photographs, to experience the charms of the quiet, willow-lined canals dotted with swans, to see the peaked bridges reflected in the dark water, and the tall, ivy-covered gables. All the magic of an idyllic Flanders lies enfolded in these picturesque attractions, enlivened today as in ages past by the ringing of the ancient carillon. These scenes lie scattered here and there waiting to be discovered: around the bend in a street that appeared to be dead-end, at the corner of a canal that had seemed rather drab.

First-time visitors are never disappointed: the city opens up for them its full store of romance and tradition. But it doesn't stop there. After living up to expectations, Bruges wins over people's hearts and imprints itself in their minds. Thus its charm gives way to enchantment.

It can happen at any moment. Someone enjoying a morning stroll might chance to notice a family of swans sculpted in relief under the blind arches in a brick facade.

Bruges wouldn't be Bruges without its canals. They range from the neat and orderly Reie (pages 2 and 3) to the bohemian Gouden Handrei (pages 6 and 7). From the top of the belfry, the facades on Steenstraat seem to unfurl, whereas the Rosaire quay and the rooftops of Wollestraat at the entrance to the Huidenvettersplein appear telescoped (opposite). Bruges is a veritable cornucopia of details. These sculpted swans (left) and statue of the Madonna and Child (above) are but a sampling of its offerings.

AMBIORIX
Restaurant
Tea-Room
Restaurant SINT-JORIS Brasserie
HOTEL-RESTAURANT "CENTRAL"

Don't let the busy line-up of outdoor cafes on the Markt keep you from noticing the beautiful red stepped gables on the square's north side (opposite). Dating from the 17th century, this group of houses was clearly designed as a unified ensemble, but successive restorations have introduced a dash of diversity – not an unhappy result. Seen from the ground, the spire of the Church of Our Lady is a most imposing sight: but from the belfry it is positively majestic against a background of flatlands that stretch southward as far as the eye can see.

A moment later, that same person might spy between two glinting, small-paned windows, a carving of the Madonna and Child on a Gothic base. In a twinkling, these visual impressions merge with others, creating a hallucinatory tangle of canals, bridges and gables. The visitor gradually realizes that this is a place where details compete with the whole for attention, and that Bruges is never as beautiful when seen through its famous mists as it is when viewed in close focus.

But before attending to the details, it's advisable to get a feeling for the whole, to observe the entire city from the top of the legendary belfry that rises above it. Because Bruges and the surrounding countryside are absolutely flat, this 83-metre-tall structure was originally of vital practical importance. It served as a watchtower for defense and fire, and as a bell tower for sounding the hours. It also provided, as it does today, an ideal vantage point from which to admire the splendors below. For what's the good of building marvels if there isn't a suitable place for contemplating them? Just as in the past, the city's dramatic observation deck is reached by means of a narrow staircase that spirals up to the top of the tower.

The first glance at the panoramic view persuades one that the climb has been more than worthwhile. The Flemish countryside stretches out in all directions around the city, which seems to huddle within it as if surrounded by a giant green moat. Surprisingly, the canals are inconspicuous, drowned in a sea of rooftops and walls. Lost too in the (bird's-seye) view are the distinct characters of individual neighborhoods. From on high, the architecture looks totally homogeneous.

Keen on ornamentation, Bruges residents often decorate rooftops and the points of gables with sculptures cast in lead. These houses on the Markt are crowned with a bestiary that includes species ranging from the Burgundian snail to a fairy-tale mermaid (above).

The most unexpected discovery lies elsewhere, to the north. Even knowing that Bruges is just a few miles from the sea, the significance of that distance cannot be fully understood until it is visualized. Its importance can be summarized as a paradox: the city is too close to the sea not to be drawn to it – in other words, Bruges is too maritime not to entertain seafaring ambitions – but at the same time it is too far away to function as a major port. Land-locked maritime city or inland coastal city, call it what you will: either way, its contradictory nature is a function of its ambiguous geographical position – which is, uncomfortably, neither here nor there. Some consider it untenable.

Bruges' entire history would seem to confirm that opinion. As long as the Zwin, a natural tributary, linked Bruges to the coast, it functioned as the city's umbilical cord. However, the river was neither wide nor deep enough to last long. Gradually it silted up until sometime in the 15th century it became completely unnavigable. That marked the beginning of Bruges' long decline, which lasted until the turn of the 20th century. Its resurgence came with the development of Zeebrugge, a modern port that can be seen from the belfry, in the distance to the north. Zeebrugge is linked to Bruges by the Baudoin Canal, which goes right to the outskirts of the city and is lined with docks that can accommodate medium-sized ships carrying everything from kiwis and bananas to Japanese cars.

Vivid traces still remain of the grandeur of the Middle Ages, when Bruges' importance as a port placed it just behind Paris, ahead of London and in rivalry with Genoa and Florence. That was the glorious era that shaped the city and endowed it with a taste for refinement which it would never lose.

Some people prefer to ignore or refuse to accept the simple truth that

Steenstraat, between the Markt (Market Square) and the Zand esplanade, is one of the busiest commercial thoroughfares in Bruges. Formerly the city's main street, it is lined with handsome buildings – some of them veritable palaces. These were originally owned by the guilds, which attempted to out-do each other in architectural grandiosity (right). The Masons' guild hall was restored in time to impress audiences of the 2002 cultural festivities, as was the facade of the old Clerk's Office on the Burg (opposite, above).

Behind the Church of Our Lady and beside the picturesque St. Boniface Bridge, the splayed branches of espaliered lime trees are supported on lattices. Meticulous attention to the urban environment is a key source of Bruges' special charm. How much would be lost without the ubiquitous, colorfully planted flowerboxes!

treasures of art and architecture are always material translations of economic and political power. Especially in architecture, nothing great or beautiful has ever been created without this kind of backing and incentive. In the case of Bruges, as long as its wealth and power prevailed, palaces, churches and mansions were put up that reflected the city's exalted standing. But as soon as the city's fortunes tumbled, all else followed, and nothing further of note was built. Bruges architects devoted their efforts to restoring the brilliant remains of a bygone era to their former splendor.

There is every reason to think that if, rather than hurtling into a precipitous decline, Bruges had maintained its preeminence, its face would have been greatly altered: the regularity of its features would surely have been marred irreparably. Instead of a harmonious city reflecting the opulence and pageantry of the Renaissance that produced it, we would have to settle for an agglomeration of disparate relics and a mixture of clashing styles. Plainly stated, if we owe Bruges' splendor to its long period of ascendancy, we owe the felicities of its current state to its collapse. Having lain transfixed as if in deep sleep, its past has been relatively easy to recover. The crisis that hit Bruges bears comparison to the one that buried Pompeii under the ashes of Vesuvius. Both cities were emptied of their living substance, but had they not been, we would probably have only a vague notion of their extraordinary beauty.

Pearl of Flanders, Athens of the Low Countries, Venice of the North, Venice in Black...none of these monikers is worthy of Bruges, whose name is so evocative of mist and bricks, muses and sea breezes – but not sailors. It comes from the Norman "bryggia," meaning "pontoon" or "pier," and sums

The same fastidious care goes into maintaining the almshouses, which are to Bruges what the scuole are to Venice: concentrations of the local spirit. The almshouses of Meulenaere, at the corner of Nieuwe Gentweg and de Groeninge, first opened in 1613 (above).

up the city's destiny in a single word. Its aptness should suffice, making comparisons superfluous. Why reduce Bruges to a dubious metonym? The label "Pearl of Flanders" conveys the notion of a fossilized, museum city. "Athens of the Lowlands," as Erasmus called it, evokes the era when Bruges, approaching its heyday, drew lessons from the ancient Greeks. Predictably, its canals invite comparisons to Venice, and perhaps thankfully it is not alone in this respect: Amsterdam and Stockholm also share the misleading title "Venice of the North." Bruges and Venice diverge not only in their striking differences in size and in latitude, but in almost every respect. Venice is a city marked by theatricality and extravagance, whereas Bruges is one of suggestive half-tones, and its celebrations more closely resemble village fairs than masked balls. It would be fairer to compare Bruges to Treviso, its true counterpart in the Veneto. In fact, Bruges is less a Venice of the north than Treviso is a Bruges of the south. As for Baudelaire's "Venice in Black," it mostly suits Symbolist fantasy. That is the reason why the author of *The Flowers of Evil* made it the imaginary destination of his poem "Invitation to the Voyage," whose verses introduce each of the this book's chapters.

These 12th-century steps on Sint Annarei (above) and the Koningstraat bridge straddling the canal near the Jan Van Eyckplein siphon (right) are eloquent embodiments of the nostalgia that abides in many parts of the city, notably in the eastern section.

My child, my sister, dream
How sweet all things would seem
Were we in that kind land to live together.

Other frequently used epithets aren't much better. "Bruges the Beautiful" is passable, if redundant, but "*Bruges-la-Morte*" (Bruges the Dead) just doesn't do. Jules Michelet's unjust term was adopted for the title of Georges Rodenbach's 19th-century novel, and thus became popular. This would lead one to believe

One of the most magical places in Bruges is the Walplein (above), where many of the city's lacemakers used to live and work. The past is almost palpable in this little square, whose resonant atmosphere has not been lost on the city's coachmen. They include it unfailingly on their horse-drawn tours.

that the label may have held more than a grain of truth at that time, and that the liveliness described by the contemporary novelist Dominique Rolin in her *Bruges la Vive* is a recent phenomenon.

In fact, it seems that Bruges acquired its seductive vocation only in the late 1970s, when, having rediscovered the marvels of its golden age, the West Flanders capital resolved to make the best of them. Ever since, these precious relics have been fastidiously preserved as so many tourist attractions. It wasn't long ago that Bruges had few foreign visitors. The British would come at Easter, attracted by a few fine restaurants and congenial pubs, and French families would join the Procession of the Holy Blood on the Feast of the Ascension. In just two decades, all that has changed. The lethargic city has been transformed into a major tourist destination. With nearly four million visitors a year, Bruges is recognized today as a gem of European cultural heritage. Its designation as European Cultural Capital for 2002 comes as a well-deserved acknowledgement of its achievement in reviving its invaluable assets.

Residents of Bruges, *Bruggelingen* in Dutch, have grown accustomed to starry-eyed romantic travelers, just as the residents of Salzburg have got used to music lovers and those of Florence to connoisseurs of art and architecture. They have learned to live with, and sometimes for, these visitors. It isn't unusual to see the most obliging of residents lingering on their front steps, maps in hand, directing tourists who have lost their way.

Travelers may have little time or desire for guidance by *Bruggelingen*, but the latter are certainly able to help them make the most of their wanderings.

The natives – especially the most sensitive among them, the ones attuned to the play of light and changing atmosphere – know where to listen for the city's secret melody, where to breathe in its hidden fragrance and where to grasp its mystery. They know how to find inspiration in the sea breezes and perhaps even, by experience, have mastered the technique of being won over subconsciously by the unique, stimulating spirit of Bruges, of surrendering to its enchantment.

Around this venerable old bridge, the camera's lense has captured a delightfully composed landscape worthy of Corot.

ALONG THE CANALS

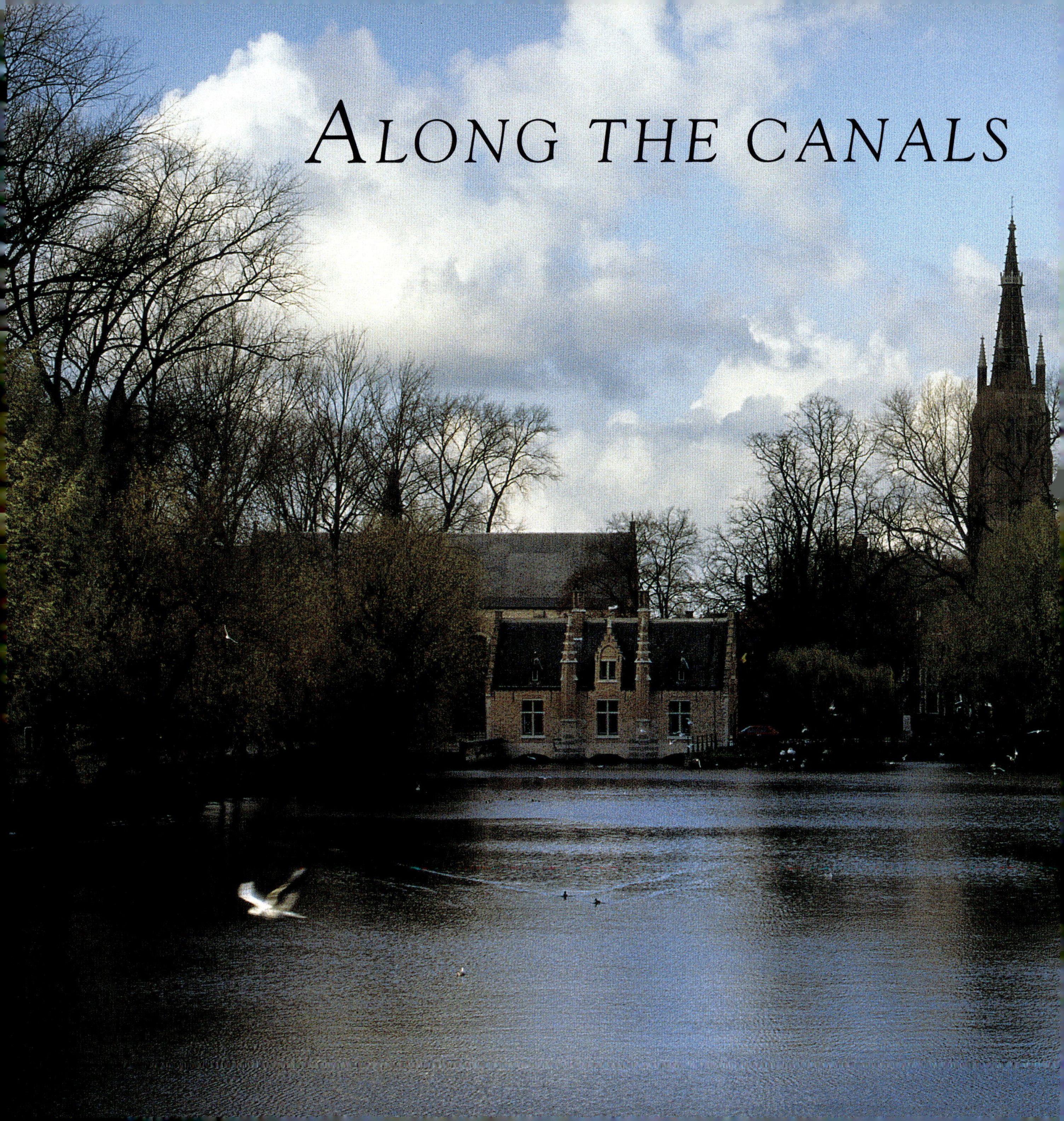

ALONG THE CANALS

See, sheltered from the swells
There in the still canals
Those drowsy ships that dream of sailing forth.

From the last writings on parchment to the earliest photographs, historic documents describe Bruges as a place thronged with heavily laden, high-masted ships. There can be no doubt that such a strong naval presence gave the city an atmosphere much different – more active, more open – than the one we know today. Now, except for a handful of barges on the outskirts and occasional police boats in the center, the only vessels that ply the canals are large, open craft fitted with benches from which passengers can observe marvel upon marvel passing by on either side.

In early times, ships approached Bruges from the northeast, on the artificial prolongation of the Zwin river known as the Reie. They dropped anchor in a catchment basin located on the site of the present lake Minnewater, where, after the Ghent canal opened in 1614, they were joined by barges arriving on that waterway from the south. Interestingly, the name "Minnewater" can be translated to mean "Lake of Love" or "Devil's Lake." Supposedly, the tragic heroine Minna is buried beneath its still waters. The story goes that this daughter of a Saxon pirate fell madly in love with the handsome Morin Stromberg. Her choice

The inscription over the monumental entrance to the Begijnhof De Wijngaard (Beguinage of the Vinyard) (opposite) consists of the single word: "Refuge." That motto would be appropriate to the whole admirably preserved, tranquil site of Minnewater. The arches of the old bridge (left), the sleepy waters of the lake, the ancient trees and the swans that have made it their domain conspire to make this a consummately romantic spot. The steeples seen in the distance only add to its charm (pages 20 and 21).

North of the lake, the Lock Keeper's House (right), built in the 16th century, looks like a miniature version of the famous French Chateau Chenonceaux, which straddles the Loire River. Like that structure, this one was designed for strategic purposes, and it recalls Minnewater's early role as a port. In the days when a chain gate and two tall towers barred access to its southern end from the direction of Ghent, this wide section of the Reie accommodated whole flotillas of commercial and passenger barges. In 1745, during the second campaign of Flanders, Louis XV and his son berthed here. The records don't say whether or not the two royals stopped in at the beguinage, which can be seen from the lake through the foliage (opposite).

displeased her father, who, by ignoring her passion seems to have sealed her fate. Minna fled to the forest, where she spent many days and nights pining for her lover. When at last he found her weeping beside a stream, it was too late: he kissed her as she breathed her last. Crazed with sorrow, Stromberg diverted the stream from its course and buried Minna in its channel. Then he restored the water to its bed and let it flow over her grave. Ever since then, local Tristans and Iseults have gravitated to this place to measure the force of their own budding passions.

Familiarity with local legends and history is indispensable if one wishes to understand a city such as this, which offers as much to the imagination as it does to the eye. Bruges is first and foremost a vast stage set where fantasy, stimulated by vestiges of the past that have been burnished and elaborated over centuries, combines with history. For example, there's the story from the ninth century of Baldwin Iron-Arm, the first Count of Flanders, who after eloping with Judith, daughter of Charles the Bald, rescued her from the claws of a ferocious bear on the very spot where Bruges would later be founded. In 1302 the Flemish nobility and commoners joined forces to defend themselves against the invading army of the French King, Philip the Fair, and pitted their foot soldiers against the might of the French cavalry. The underdogs emerged victorious, carrying five hundred golden spurs taken from their foe. If tales of exploits such as these don't send a little shiver down your spine, you risk missing much of the thrill that the city has to offer.

Bruges has been marked physically by every chapter of its history. Thus, a walk along its canals is like a walk through time. The powerful counts of Flanders ringed the city with fortifications; the hoisting gear that traders in the Middle

At its terminus, the old Reie canal, which linked Bruges to the Zwin and thus to the sea, is framed by the Spinolarei and Spiegelrei embankments, with their beautifully ordered rows of 17th-century houses. A few steps beyond the Poorters' loge, which is distinguishable by its tower (above), the water channels underground and disappears from sight beneath Jan Van Eyckplein and Vlamingstraat.

Flemish gables and Neo-classical exteriors face off in a battle of style at the corner of Verversdijk and Spinolarei. But the adversaries' differences are blurred and their architectural dispute mooted by their reflections in the still waters of the canal (right). A bit farther along on Verversdijk, the combined effect of the stepped gables' pure lines, the continuous crenelated chain that results from their uninterrupted juxtapositions, their mullions and square window panes is one of incomparable beauty (pages 30 and 31).

As in most cities, the farther from the centre one goes, the more breathing space one finds. That explains why the houses on the Langerei have more elbow room than their counterparts in the heart of Bruges. The urban environment is less dense here, and conducive to refreshing walks.

Ages installed in attics and the windows they added to basements are still visible along the canals. It was under the Dukes of Burgundy, who acquired the province as part of a marriage settlement in 1384, that the city received its flamboyant palaces, among them the guild-houses of the Porters, who, as their name suggests, were professional stevedores, and the Poorters, a group of privileged merchants not to be confused with porters. The buildings of both are on Jan Van Eyckplein.

The other thing that must be kept firmly in mind while getting acquainted with Bruges is the illusory nature of much of the city's charm. Here, if a building is said to date from the 16th century, it means that its origins and the style of its architecture and decorative elements are indeed from that era. But as for the actual stones, they are most likely of a more recent, 19th or even 20th-century vintage. Many of these landmarks have been restored or reconstructed to such a degree that nothing, or next to nothing, remains of their original structures. In effect, the pages of history that Bruges summons us to step into are largely a rebuilt illusion, elaborated on a most impressive scale.

Bruges' romantic aspect tends to eclipse its inherent strangeness. The city's double nature, mineral and aquatic, is the cause of many a bizarre perception. The images of dark eyes formed by the reflected surbased arches of some 80 bridges have inspired more than a few poems.

Unfortunately, Bruges' erstwhile identity as a port city – a medieval trading centre affiliated to the Hanseatic League – goes largely underappreciated by most of today's visitors. It would be a shame to lose touch with that bustling, cosmopolitan aspect of the city's past. People of 17 nationalities rented rooms in the boarding house known as Ter Beurse, from which the "Bourse" stock exchange acquired its name. Nearby, the Florentines' abode still retains original parts of its handsome facade. Just a stone's throw beyond, beside the Spinolarei,

is the place where the sea channel flowed abruptly out of sight beneath the embankment. Here, near what remains of the old wharf, is where one should imagine a slew of boats unloading English wool and northern timber, and taking on Flemish textiles and bolts of cloth as well as spices transported overland from the East.

The Burgundian period, which left more tangible traces, has become nearly synonymous with the lavish wedding celebrations and jousting tournaments that were among the hallmarks of the city's golden age under the regimes of Philip the Bold, Charles the Bold and Philip the Good. It was then that the Order of the Golden Fleece convened in the choir of Saint Saviour's Cathedral, where the members' coats of arms and the memory of their exploits are still carefully preserved.

Nowhere are the city's Burgundian accents more palpable than in the vast precincts of the Halles – originally the Cloth Market – at the foot of the belfry. Crossing this cavernous, slope-roofed interior court at nightfall is one of the headiest experiences that Bruges has to offer to visitors with a taste for medieval grandeur.

Then Spain stepped in, and like Burgundy before it, left traces of its passage, although the remains of Spain's domination are less salient and more scattered. The Spanish Habsburgs' imprint is neither particularly conspicuous nor ever entirely absent in the city whose decline was cushioned by these occupiers from the south. If Charles V's spirit is still detectable here and there, a discerning eye is needed to find it in an austere facade with high windows or in a monumental door surmounted by a baroque pediment. A great number of forms and styles overlap so comfortably and mix so well into the kaleidoscopic whole that it is

It's impossible to get to know Bruges by car. Walking, or as Bruge denizens themselves prefer, cycling (opposite), are the only means of transport that enable visitors to absorb the poetry of the canals. In either case, it's crucial to be observant of the smallest details, such as the bicephalous Flemish lions which support miles of handrailings (above).

futile for first-time visitors to try to clear up too neatly the confusion of feelings and impressions that mount as they explore the canals. It's far better to let it all simply sink in.

Bruges is never lovelier than on a dry, chilly day in the spring or fall, when the low sun shines brilliantly through the clear air. That's the weather best suited to this flat landscape – the weather depicted in the backgrounds of Van Eyck and Roger Van der Weyden. Under these atmospheric conditions, the gables of Bruges stand out clearly against the limpid sky, acquiring a timeless and somehow comforting strangeness in the pale light. This is the perfect moment to give in to the desire to take a boat ride on the canals, which are more welcoming and familiar than they may appear initially. It would be easy, and untrue, to claim that the only way to discover Bruges is by boat. But it should be admitted that although the city holds many other pleasures, none of them is as immediate as a tour on the canals.

The incomparably beautiful Rosaire quay, with its stately old homes and gardens that seem to float on the surface of the canal, makes an ideal setting for the Ducs de Bourgogne Hotel (above). The belfry's tall tower silhouetted against the brooding Flemish sky only adds to the magic (opposite). This lyrical spirit's counterpoint is found in the tall, spare facades of Spiegelrei (pages 38 and 39).

Observers rock back and forth between the city's stable reality and its moving reflection – its static body and its moveable soul. Here a wall ripples and becomes liquid; there a waterway ends, as if petrified. People attracted to the bizarre and strange enjoy seeing in this reversible city an entire upside-down world. "One can only know how to see the things of this world by looking at them upside down," Balthasar Gracian has written. It is tempting to add that one can only know how to see Bruges by looking at its reflection in the canals. Sometimes in the fading light the buildings and their reflections in the water join together, from one side of the quai to the other, like an immense Rorschach ink blot open to all interpretations.

In "The Object World," published in his *Critical Essays*, Roland Barthes

describes Amsterdam, but it might as well have been the Bruges of long ago, as "a water-merchandise complex." "It is water that makes the object," he writes, "giving it all the nuances of a calm, planar mobility, collecting supplies, shifting them without perceptible transition from one exchange to another, making the entire city into a census of agile goods." All of a sudden, it seems a great pity that the canals of Bruges are no longer used for much of anything besides tour boats.

A trip to the heart of the old city takes one back not only through time but also through styles, from Neo-classical to Romanesque by way of the Baroque and Gothic. Certain intact structures like the Westerhof (opposite) and the St. Boniface bridge (above) still possess their original medieval character, which owes much to the picturesque imbrication of forms and materials.

As the vessel threads it way between the quais, the unfolding scene of perfect order becomes a source of great delight. Everything partakes of this equilibrium, which holds the gaze between stone and water, sky and reflection, hard surfaces and lush vegetation. Wild grasses and climbing plants that attach themselves in thick clumps to the stones and find nourishment there, lend a touch of disorder and life to the canal banks and make them seem less severe. It's difficult to imagine the kind of image the watery mirror would send back if it weren't for this felicitous effect of neglect, or what the reflection would lose in charm if the flora that no one has cultivated or cared for, were to disappear. This type of errant vegetation presents a striking contrast with the expertly manicured plantings that are more typical of the city – notably the espaliered lime trees lining the perimeters of certain public squares. The purpose of these arbors is practical as well as esthetic: they create wind screens to protect the enclosed space year-round. Not only lime trees, but mosses, too, blend into the cityscape and are an integral part of it. They belong to that category of subliminal phenomena which, when brought together, create a singular atmosphere. When the eye skims over these things without necessarily registering what it sees, it gets the message that "This is Bruges."

Although the overall economic picture of Bruges was grim indeed during the 18th century, there was prosperity enough for certain families to build themselves grand houses out near the city limits. Fine examples of these homes, which were designed in the Neo-classical style then popular in France, have recently been restored in the southwest part of the city, on Speelmansrei (left), and in the northeast on Sint Annarei (right). Their architecture may not be indigenous to West Flanders, but it is no less admirable for that.

Swans too blend into the decor of this special universe. In fact, their beaks are literally inscribed with the B of Bruges. Their nonchalant presence on the canals isn't explained by esthetic considerations alone. These birds are the city's tribute to the memory of Pieter Lanchals, whose name, "lange hals," is Dutch for "long neck." Lanchals was a close associate of the Archduke Maximilian of Austria and was a victim of the 1488 uprising in which the people of Bruges lashed out against the archduke and his oppressive policies. To avenge his friend's death, Maximilian imposed upon the city the bizarre penalty of harboring swans. The people of Bruges seem not to have minded in the least, nor have the swans, which over centuries have appeared quite content to stay. Even the tourist boats don't ruffle their feathers.

All up and down the canals, each embankment has its own name, with the result that opposite sides of the same canal have separate identities. Strung like unmatching yet perfectly fitted beads along the waterways, the houses are precisely juxtaposed, with each distinguished from its neighbors yet integral to the ensemble. What's more, the greater a building's singularity, the better it seems to fit in. Visions of orderly successions of variously shaped gables leap to mind long after visitors have left Bruges.

The most authentic Flemish homes – or at least the ones that have best retained their integrity – could be those standing on the quiet banks of Sint-Annarei and Potterierei. Theirs is not the romantic charm of medieval or Renaissance dwellings. Rather, they emit a lofty classicism that is most tellingly

expressed in their noble, sparingly ornamented facades, which resemble those of the town houses of Amsterdam. Visitors rarely venture into this eastern part of the old city, and that's a pity, for this is an ideal place – far from tourist attractions – to take the pulse of the real Bruges and get a feeling for its true personality. Here, it's still possible to meet the Flemish "at home" – upon invitation, naturally.

There is no way to force friendship upon the people of Bruges. Like the city itself, which shelters behind high walls, they resist revealing too much too quickly. From the Burgundians they adopted the custom of displaying their worldly goods behind closed doors. Sightseers are often amazed to catch sight of luxuriant bowers and marvellous architecture behind austere portals. And what is true of the outside is even truer of the interiors of these houses, particularly since the city has become a tourist destination.

Photographers have always gravitated to Groenerei (Green Quay) on the outskirts of Bruges' historic centre, both for its own features and for the heady views it offers of the city's towers – most notably, the belfry (above).

Faced with the large influx of visitors, Bruges residents have taken pains to preserve their privacy. Here the Flemish penchant for transparency, which in other parts of the region makes living rooms appear like display cases that reveal all about the unmysterious lives conducted within, yields to curtains and lace work that block the view. The only way to see these interiors is by being invited in. Then one can admire at leisure the black and white floor tiles, shiny with wear; the ivory-laquered, turned-wood bannisters; chandeliers with their spheres of

Nowhere is the ambience more bewitching than here, where Viane, the main protagonist in Bruges-la-Morte, imagines that he hears a murmuring voice rising from the water (left). The hexagonal gazebo that overhangs the canal is one of the elegant tea pavilions that sprouted in fashionable gardens during the 18th century (opposite, below). Although by then it had been cut off from the sea, Bruges retained a predilection for exotic plants – tea being foremost among them.

Drawbridges were built on the most heavily used canals to permit the passage of tall-framed boats and barges piled high with cargo. The one shown here is situated north of Langerei, not far from the port of Damme, one of the city's seven gates. Its simple but imposing structure conveys a notion of the bustling activity that went on here six hundred years ago.

gleaming copper; artfully arranged colocynths – the same furnishings that Vermeer painted, and made familiar to us all.

As has already been mentioned, the people of Bruges tend to be aloof – it takes a long time to win their confidence. But once secured, it remains unshakeable. As for their supposed disdain for outsiders, that reputation dates back decades to the city's fallow days and no longer holds true, for things have changed. Today Bruges is moving forward on the European stage. New, open elites are forming, and concentrations of young talent are springing up everywhere in the city and its vicinity.

Among all of Bruges' many treasures, the canals constitute the city's most remarkable and unique contribution to the cultural heritage of Europe. These views of Carmersburg (opposite) and Langerei (above), whose compositions appear to be inspired by Impressionism and Cubism respectively, give an idea of the evocative power of their subjects.

Bruges' homogeneous social fabric has facilitated its renewed embrace of tourism and culture.

Throughout history, middle- and working-class citizens have lived together in the same neighborhoods, and in the same homes. The consequence of this symbiosis is the visible fact that Bruges does not divide up neatly into rich and poor neighborhoods. Opulent residences almost always rub shoulders with those of a more modest, albeit invariably dignified, character. Indeed, a general state of dignity accounts for the solidarity of Bruges' widely diversified stock of citizens. It has always been so. It's impossible to imagine Bruges without the Flemish virtues of reserve, courtesy, and helpfulness which created it. It's impossible to imagine Bruges without its *Bruggelingen* (residents).

Certain things are simply too precious to be abandoned even after they have become obsolete. For the benefit of the material historical record and the local tourist industry, Bruges has preserved examples of its disused but still much-loved antique machinery. On the circular canal that surrounds the city, old barges (below left) and a few rare windmills (left and opposite) attract the interest of young children and their elders alike. The Bonne Chiere and St. John windmills pictured here are two of the four power-generators of their kind that have survived out of a total of around 30 which used to operate in the area.

BRUGGE
DJAZ

LE F
Grill
Rest

BRICKS AND STONES

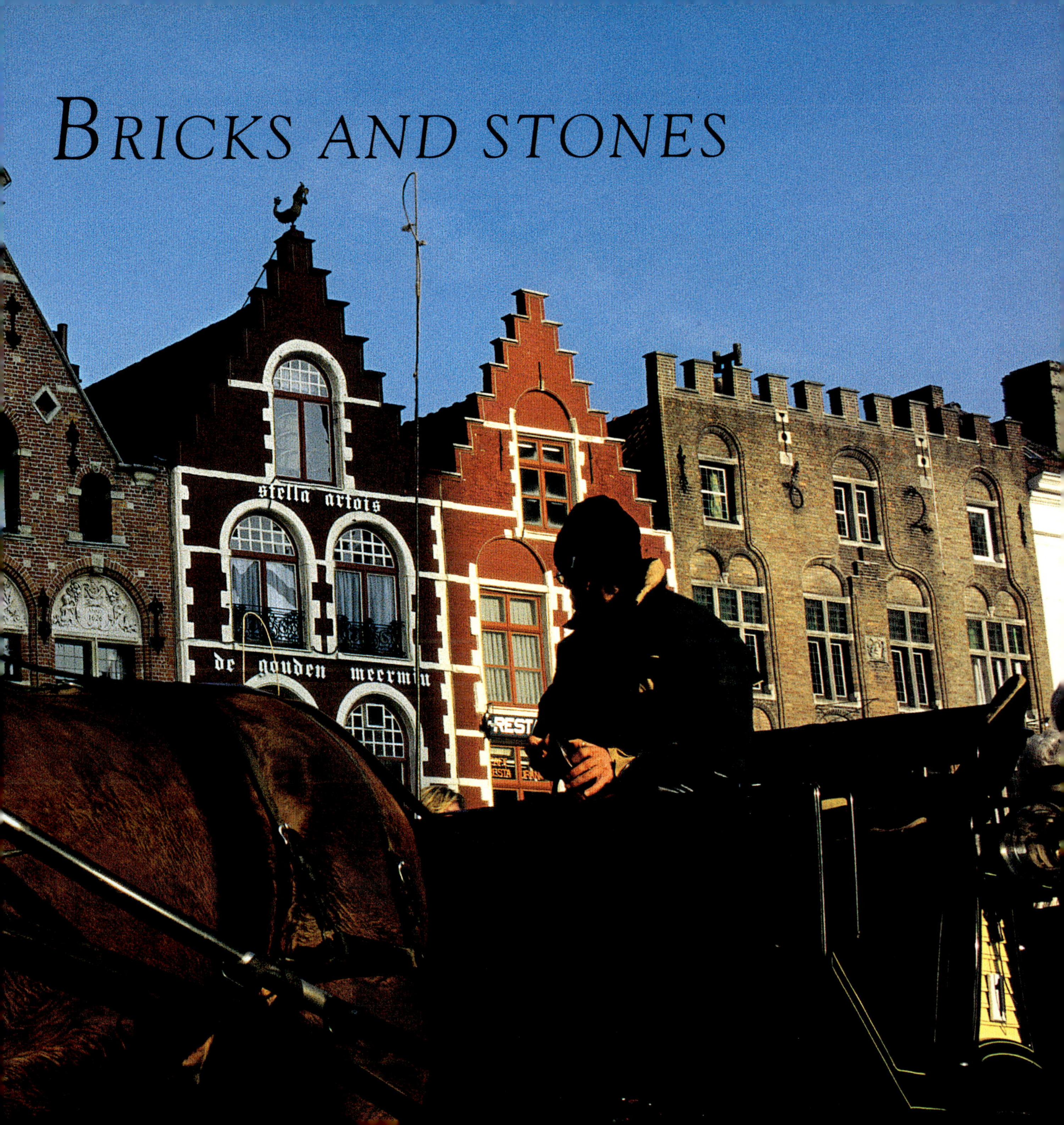

BRICKS AND STONES

Nothing but should address
The soul's loneliness,
Speaking her sweet and secret native tongue.

The best way to get to know Bruges is by surveying its marvels at leisure, using intuition as a guide. Let your steps take you across lively squares or along quiet, winding streets whose routes are sometimes circular, leading you back to where you began. Feeling one's way is an ideal means of getting acquainted with a city so rich in visual surprises. It's a capricious place, and there is much pleasure to be had in giving oneself over to its charm. Like many other cities that have retained their medieval foundations, Bruges teems with narrow lanes, nooks and passages. Many of its finest jewels are also its least conspicuous, to the great joy of visitors who wander off the beaten track. Many surprises await them – happy results of the city's unplanned urban structure: a beautiful, tall house at the end of the modest Oude Zomerstraat seems to have taken root at the wrong address; a splendid view of the canal and of the picturesque Ducs de Bourgogne Hotel opens up at the end of a dark, vaulted passage called Cross of Burgundy. Visitors who lose their way in Bruges are certain to make discoveries and be richly rewarded with surprises. What greater satisfactions could an urban explorer hope for?

The belfry that towers over the old Cloth Market was reconstructed in the 14th century after being destroyed by fire. An octagonal storey was added to it at the end of the 15th century, and it received its Neo-Gothic crown only in 1822 (above). In the same square, the regional capitol building's Neo-gothic facade serves as a dramatic backdrop for a monument to the Bruges Matins (left). Stepped gables enliven the square's north side (pages 52 and 53, and opposite). The Markt by night, aglow with light, is a spectacle in itself.

LE PANIER D'OR

Huidenvettersplein (Tanners Square) is named for the Tanners Guild, which used to occupy this brick building with its beautiful Baroque gable (right). Many doorways are surmounted by ornately carved bas-reliefs inscribed with the date of the building's construction (below).

The restored exterior of Ter Beurse, which was erected on Vlamingstraat, near the Italians' loge, in the 14th century, exemplifies the "third type" of Flemish Renaissance style and is quite modern in appearance. Traders and financial brokers from all over Europe met here to wheel and deal. "Ter Beurse" literally became the "bourse," or stock exchange.

In order to prolong the magic of a walk through Bruges, it's best not to try too hard to disentangle the myriad of impressions that accumulate, but rather, allow them to coalesce. This enables one to focus on the big question: What is the essence of this city's beauty? One of the best spots for pondering the matter is the Huidenvettersplein, or Tanners Square, whose heterogeneity fascinates even the most blase traveler. The low reliefs adorning the facade of the *Auberge de la Vache*, for example, illustrate various aspects of leather-working. Such refined skills brought to such mundane subjects! The city's beauty is practically tangible here. If this site is beheld in a single glance, the clean lines, the heavy masses, dense materials and matte surfaces of the ensemble appear to have been composed to embody the very notion of beauty, to allow it to be contemplated in its most concrete form.

Set into a niche on the facade of the Poorters Loge, this ursine figure holding an escutcheon in its paws recalls the heroic deed of Baldwin Iron-Arm, the First Count of Flanders, on the site where Bruges was to be founded.

Stone cartouches ornamented with initials, symbols, dates and dedicatory inscriptions mark exterior walls throughout the city. While scholars may be able to decode their forgotten meanings, the rest of us can enjoy their readily appreciable beauty. The detail shown in the top photograph is from Vlamingstraat; the one above from Oude Burg.

Esthetically, the true secret of this city is that everything, from the Basilica of the Holy Blood to the humblest of chapels, is designed to human scale. Like these structures, whose measurements were plotted in "hands" and "feet" and which owe their forms and proportions to the physical dimensions of their makers, Bruges, at least in its historic centre, preserves in its stones the imprint of those who built it.

The respect shown by the people of Bruges for the work of their forebears is linked to the impression the city gives of belonging to pre-industrial times. One only has to look closely at the hand-forged street lamps to appreciate the resistance of local taste to modern standardization. Banal aluminum lighting fixtures, so common everywhere else, don't stand a chance of invading this city.

What we so much enjoy in Bruges, and what many visitors come in quest of without consciously being aware of it, is the absence of visual pollution. For

generations, the town fathers have admitted little in the way of up-to-date urban accessories. None of the billboards, illuminated signs or neon lights that have become part of the urban landscape everywhere else can be found here. To be acceptable for display, advertising must be discreet and signage unplugged and integrated into the surroundings. No unnecessary urban furnishings spoil the look of the old centre, and no unsightly bit of infrastructure disfigures it. In Bruges, urban development takes a back seat to the preservation of cultural heritage. Even when it came to readying the city for its role as a European cultural capital, this wisdom prevailed and moderation reigned.

The same policy has seen the expansion of pedestrian zones and the banishing of most cars to parking lots on the periphery of the old city. The change in atmosphere effected by this small revolution is particularly striking on the Market Square (*Markt*), for example, which used to be clogged with automobiles and is now free of them.

In the silence that has returned to the heart of the city, the cobbled streets seem to resound more loudly with the clip-clopping of horses' hoofs. And indeed they do. More one-horse carriages than ever before in living memory now ply the city streets. Not all of them of course, can honestly be described as masterfully restored antiques, but all of them contribute a picturesque note and invoke a certain nostalgia. There is no more romantic way of exploring Bruges than from the seat of one of these carriages.

Fortunately, they are equipped with hoods, for it rains frequently. Showers disrupt very little here just because they are so common. Flemish drizzle is easy to live with because one gets used to it and is always prepared for it. After all, this is the land of shimmer and reflection, of scintillating surfaces that mask

Just as Hans Memling (whose statue is shown at left) depicted them, the municipal buildings of Bruges are a tour de force of the style known as Flamboyant Gothic. Outstanding among them is the town hall, a jewel of 16th-century architecture with its tall windows surmounted by openwork tympanums, its statues mounted on canopied bases, its arced friezes and corbeled towers (right). Sculpture and gilding enliven the exteriors of Renaissance buildings, such as the old Clerk's Office, which is now the Brugse Vrije Museum (opposite, bottom), as well as those of the Baroque era, like the Masons' Guildhall on Steenstraat (opposite, top).

In a flat city such as Bruges, the importance of bell towers is compounded by the fact that they constitute the sole vertical elements in the urban landscape. The one atop the Church of Jerusalem was erected in the 15th century by the Adornes, a Genoan merchant family based in Bruges. Its golden dome was meant to recall the family's pilgrimage to the Church of the Holy Sepulcher in the Holy Land (above).

The tall tower of St. Savior's Cathedral is a jumble of styles. The first floor was built on Roman foundations at the turn of the 13th century. The Gothic third storey, which was completed only in the 17th century, was destroyed by fire in 1839. That tragedy necessitated the rebuilding of the steeple, whose style is Neo-romanesque. Purer architectural strains are represented by the medieval tower of the Guildhall of the Archers of St. Sebastian (upper right) and the Baroque dome of the English Convent (lower right). A concern for esthetics is evident everywhere in Bruges. Consider, for instance, the handsome brick facades – some left their natural color, others painted yellow – on Oude Burg (pages 62 and 63).

The oculi and low-relief carvings that adorn the gables of the old houses have but one raison d'etre, and that is visual pleasure (above). Respectful of the refinements of its past, the city is careful to preserve them. Most of the street lamps, for example, are 19th-century originals of wrought iron and moulded glass. The only concession made to modernity as far as they are concerned has been their conversion to electricity (right). Each lamp post is crowned by a stylized rampart with seven doors, representing the seven gates of the city.

Over the centuries, the decorative elements on the buildings of Bruges have been carefully preserved. This delicate tracery on a Gothic facade on Oude Burg (below) is remarkably intact. The same is true of a bow window added in the 18th century to a gable on Langerei (upper right) and of a trio of typanums with reliefs representing Faith, Hope, and Charity at number 28 on the Markt.

underlying substance. Bruges' celebrated painters recognized this and captured it by applying transparent glazes over their representations of common objects. The resulting effulgence belies the ordinary material essence of things. It's all in the way they hold and echo back the thin light of Flanders.

Just as southerners seem instinctively to know where to find or how to create coolness and shade, and desert-dwellers know how to make the most of the slightest bit of moisture, northerners, for whom scarce light is precious, are past masters in the art of capturing, reflecting and mirroring its rays. Just enter any living room in Bruges after sunset to appreciate the inhabitants' gift for domestic lighting. The entire interior seems planned around it. Artfully placed to obtain the effects desired, lamps perfectly suited to the decorative scheme cast haloes and illuminate the space as if by degrees, creating an ambience as subtle as the ones conjured up by the Old Masters.

The wish to make the feeblest ray of light shine brightly, partly explains the local proclivity for enlivening the facades of buildings. No one criticized as gaudy, for instance, the fresh paint and gilding applied to certain prominent exteriors in the run-up to 2002. And yet, the watchdogs of authenticity are legion in Bruges, and they objected that the city was being dressed up for cultural capitaldom like a village bride. Thus the newly burnished facades of the masons' guild-house on Steenstraat and the Brugse Vrije on Burgplein make one think of Flemish tapestries – rich and heavy, with their gold and silver threads weighing down and stiffening the woven motif.

Nevertheless, the pigment and gold leaf only serve to highlight the rich sculptural ornamentation that is so characteristic of Bruges facades. The Flamboyant Gothic style of many of the major municipal buildings is less a legacy of the extravagant early medieval courts than it is a reflection of the natural tendency of the city's artists to "enflame" their materials – in this case, stone, but also, elsewhere, wood and metal.

The people of Bruges are renown decorators, or at least ornamentors, and a certain theatricality is inherent in their architecture. You don't have to go farther than Vlamingstraat, between the Markt and Jan Van Eyckplein, to deduce from the facades that in all periods of time and in all styles, this city has been an enthusiastic promotor of ornamentation and has embellished its buildings with as much of it as their structures could bear: elaborate masonry, blind arcades, friezes, sculptural reliefs, moldings and gables of every shape and size. Bruges' taste for the decorative goes as high as the rooftops, which make good perches for sculptural bestiaries. If you look up at the corner of Steenstraat and Markt, you will see a family of gold-painted lead snails perched on top of an elegant mansion's dormer windows.

Still more noticeable – and famous for other reasons – are the small statues of the Virgin Mary that seem to spring up everywhere, especially along the route of the Procession of the Holy Blood. Predominantly Roman Catholic and Marian, orientations that long ago caused problems with the neighboring United Provinces, Bruges is generously populated with these endearing sculptures that, from porch roofs and house corners, bless all who pass before them. Although they date from many periods and come in all styles, they share a single function. These protective Bruges madonnas keep watch over street

Foreign influences – some explicit, others subtle – can be found in the architecture of Bruges. They are especially easy to spot in the designs of windows and doorways. This rather austere entrance to a house in the beguinage, closely relates to the puritan style of 17th-century England (opposite, above); the carefree grace of 18th-century France shows through in the ironwork of this house on Sint Annarei (right); and the insistent Baroque design of this 19th-century entry on Predikherenstraat (opposite left) could be interpreted as a late tribute to the Spanish Habsburgs.

A statue of Saint Elizabeth welcomes visitors to the Begijnhof De Wijngaard (Beguinage of the Vineyard) (right). Sculptural likenesses of her cousin, the Virgin Mary, proliferate all over the city in richly ornamented niches carved into the exterior walls or corners of buildings. There are about 700 of these little statues in total, in styles ranging from Early Renaissance to Neo-baroque. Nothing is as delightful as catching sight of one of these miraculous apparitions in a place where you would least expect to find it.

corners and canal crossings in the same way that an army of angels watches over the heavenly Jerusalem.

It wouldn't be farfetched to assert that the most important element in the architecture of Bruges is the facade. Indeed, the Flemish consider the facade as *the* essential feature of a building. Sometimes, the facade goes up before the rest of the house and looks forlornly like an outsized stage flat that wouldn't fit into the theater; at other times, it manages to stay up when the rest of the building it was attached to is destroyed.

The notion of a house as a status symbol might well have originated in Flanders, where facades are an art form in the same way that roofing is in Burgundy and door frames are in Spain. This is especially true for Renaissance houses, which connoisseurs of the local architecture divide into three periods and types, depending on the width of the pediments, the shape of the gables, and the size and position of the windows. The facade associated with the third type features narrow windows running the full length of the upper storey and thus imparting a modern look which has inspired more than a few contemporary Flemish architects.

It is fairly common to find modern elements grafted onto historic buildings in Bruges. Yet the evidence of deep respect for the structure's original form suggests that this practice constitutes more of an homage to venerable precedent than an attempt to transform it. It is as if a predetermined formalism has taken root here that persuades even the most unconventional of architects and designers to toe the line of tradition.

If we were able to carry away with us the memory of just one material – not to mention color – encountered in this city, it would surely be brick.

Indeed, almost every house is faced with it – either left raw, varnished or boldly painted. One of the great charms of unpainted facades is their shimmering cameo appearance, which is obtained by the meticulous sizing, arranging and joining of the bricks. Depending upon whether or not they form a more or less unified whole, the bricks make the walls seem to reverberate. Often their placement is determined by chromatically created patterns or simply varieties in tone.

There is no limit to the latter. Ordinarily, bricks range in color from sandy to bistre and soot black by way of infinite shades of yellow, ocre, pink, rust and brown.Some bare walls acquire a slate-gray tint; others take on a warm and appetizing color of freshly baked bread. More than anything else, it's the contrast between the shade of the bricks and the colour of the trim that makes these facades seem to stand out in relief. Thus, deep red trimming brings dramatically to the fore the same wall that recedes when paired with dark gray. In any case, doors and windows must provide sufficient contrast to hold their own against the lively brick. Bright reds and greens are preferred over muted tones, and their effectiveness as foils is often enhanced by framing them with a thin border of pure white, the same that is used around the window panes.

Few of the small glass panes in service today are originals, but detecting whether or not they are genuine is easy: old glass contains small imperfections and variations in color – small triumphs over modern standardization. Mounted

A city of facades, Bruges harbors all kinds and styles. The vast majority have gables, whether simple or complex, straight or stepped, painted or varnished, embellished or spare, dated, named, dedicated or unmarked. Small-paned windows almost always suit them better than large panes; natural pigments harmonize better than synthetic paints; brightly colored trim is more effective than white; hand-made roofing tiles are preferable to standard varieties (opposite). The beguinage, with its architectural simplicity and verdant, wooded setting (pages 72 and 73), stands in calm counterpoint to the visual excitement of the nearby cityscape.

stella artois
de gouden meermin

in lead, these remarkable survivors of the past impart a touching aspect of fragility to a facade. They seem like thin carapaces whose scales are enlivened by the reflections of passing clouds.

Bruges' painted facades display an extensive, unexpectedly epicurean range of colors. A poem remains to be written about the daring efforts made by the city's house painters – born colorists – to harmonize the shades of walls with those of ironwork, doors and windowframes. For example, they complement tomato-red walls with salt gray trim, salmon walls with blueberry trim, pistachio with cinnamon, caramel with cassis, and vanilla with chocolate. This lively and at times high-key palette is ubiquitous in Bruges, used on everything from confectioners' shops to Saint Ursula's shrine. Its pure, bold colors seem to bespeak a need to compensate for the habitual gray of the Flemish sky.

The tranquil domain of the beguinage is suffused with an almost eerie quiet (above). Only one of the houses, the St. Begge, is open to visitors (opposite). Its rustic, domestic decor conveys a vivid impression of what life must have been like in these ascetic, spiritual refuges.

Among the most remarkable painted houses are the ones originally built as homes for fishermen's families. Modelled on the same basic design used for identical purposes in the nearby towns of Damme and Lissewege, these modest, single-storey, white-washed dwellings with their sharply contrasting black shutters are clustered in the quiet neighborhood of Westmeers. The poignant atmosphere that envelops the low structures is difficult to account for at first but gradually seems to be generated in part by the funereal solemnity of the black-trimmed windows.

The same ambience, only heightened, hovers over the almshouses (*Godshuizen*), whose reduced scale and enclosed privacy concentrate the senses. These structures, whose purpose was to house the needy, were put up during

At the centre of the beguinage, which is virtually a village within the city, the little cloister with its brick well (above) and the beautiful if heavily restored Gothic house (right), seem devoted as much to nostalgia as to meditation. But that is only an impression. Today, the serenity of the beguinage is directly linked to the spirit of the Benedictine nuns who live in and run the institution.

Bruges' lean years with funds donated by civic-minded families and guilds. Just as the wealth of earlier days had bestowed upon Bruges a sumptuous architectural legacy, the hard times that followed bequeathed these charitable refuges, several of which are found in the parish of Our Lady in the south-west section of the city, near lake Minnewater. The miniature quality of these simple, peaceful havens inevitably triggers associations with children's toys – lovingly cared-for dolls' houses arranged around tiny gardens. These still-functioning institutions of the past could have been the inspiration for the utopian thinker Alphonse Allais when he fancifully proposed the idea of building cities in the countryside. They are enfolded in quiet calm – in a timeless, slightly mournful, bucolic tranquility.

Serene too are the grounds of the nearby Begijnhof Der Wijngaard, one of the many institutions of its type, called *beguinage* in French, which originated in the Low Countries. Begijnhofs were founded by women whose husbands had left to fight in the Crusades. Rather than remaining solitary, these war widows joined together to form communities governed by mutual support and spiritual purpose. Essentially lay nuns, they forged a virtuous, independent way of life that represented a major breakthrough in the liberation of women from the social shackles of the day. With the gradual obsolescence of the vocation, begijnhofs have been taken over by the Daughters of the Church, an order of Benedictine nuns who have posted discreet signs exhorting "Stilte" ("silence") all over the peaceful property. And indeed, stillness, lush vegetation and fresh air are the hallmarks of this pastoral corner of Bruges, which seems so far removed from, yet is nevertheless so close to, the bustling activity of the Markt and Burg squares.

The almshouses can often be distinguished by their monumental entry gates. Shown here are the entrances to the complexes of Meulenaere (left) and Cobrysse (above). The principal concentration of almshouses lies between the beguinage and the Church of Our Lady. The pronounced pastoral atmosphere in this section of the city is in no way diminished by this drinking trough for horses (pages 78 and 79).

La Dentellière
EETCAFÉ • RESTAURANT
La Dentellière
EETCAFÉ • RESTAURANT

The bucolic tranquility that pervades the neighbourhood of the almshouses gives but a faint hint of that which reigns inside the precincts of the hospices themselves. Meulenaere, which opened in 1613, is considered archetypal, with its white-washed houses trimmed in bottle-green and their windows curtained with lace (left and near right). The houses cluster around small gardens where flowers add a joyous note, as they do beside this arcade near the border of Astrid Park (far right).

The overarching elegance of the city is by no means undermined by its rustic accents, which in fact are cherished as welcome reminders of calm. Although Bruges is no longer the trendsetter for all of northern Europe, nearly all of its inhabitants possess innate social ease and a deep appreciation of refinement and finesse. As if blessed with native grace, they seem strangers to *faux pas* and every form of awkwardness. From its early days of world leadership and from its important role in the life of modern Flanders, Bruges has inherited and developed its identity as a capital city whose nobility is inscribed both in its historic fabric and in the hearts of its citizens. These devout, disciplined, organized and enterprising people have always given top priority to their civic obligations, and they remain ever-conscious of their urbanity – even in the country.

The harmonious masses, pure lines and measured proportions of Bruges' noble architectural heritage are as pleasing to the eye as they are to the mind. The ear too is regaled by the mellifluous pealing of bells, which contribute an

added dimension to the polyphony of gables, roofs and perfectly punctuated brick walls – well tuned planes and volumes orchestrated in a resounding hymn to Flemish culture. Such is the brilliant urban symphony of Bruges.

Several almshouses are located on the enchanting Katelijnestraat, at the very heart of this rural part of the city. As is customary, their names and founding dates are stencilled in large, sober black letters directly on the white-washed outer walls.

GODSHUIS
DE GENERALITEIT
1572
81

LIVING IN STYLE

LIVING IN STYLE

Gold ceilings would there be,
Mirrors deep as the sea,
The walls all in an Eastern splendor hung.

The most famous quay in Bruges is the prolongation of the Rosaire known as the Dijver. Willows and lime trees line its park-like banks, which are home to the College of Europe as well as to the city's major museums. A small garden at number 12 leads to the Groeninge Museum, the repository of an illustrious panorama of Flemish art from its earliest beginnings up to the present.

One of the most celebrated paintings in the collection is Jan Van Eyck's large *Madonna and Child with the Canon Joris Van der Paele*, dated 1436. Prized for its marvelous blend of humanism and spirituality, the picture also bespeaks – just as ingeniously – the fondness for luxury that for so long has been characteristic of the people of Bruges. Never have material richness and refined *facture* been better expressed than they are here, in the Virgin's green-lined robe, in St. Donatian's stunning brocade of blue moire interwoven with gold thread, in St. George's silver-gilt armor, which reflects the scene of which it is a part, in the intense colors of the woven silk carpet and the carved alabaster throne framed by porphyry columns. With the aim of glorifying the Virgin and Child – along

A garden path leads to the entrance of the Groeninge Museum (left), whose highly prized collection includes Jan Van Eyck's masterpiece The Madonna and Child with the Canon Joris Van der Paele (opposite). The painting's splendor and refinement epitomize the fondness and fascination for luxury that the people of Bruges have shown for many centuries. The beautiful furnishings exhibited in the Gruuthuse Museum (above) and the marvelous antique lace borders of fine linen handkerchiefs (pages 84 and 85) constitute other manifestations of this proclivity.

The opulent ironwork of this sign at the entrance to the Gruuthuse Museum is a fitting symbol for a building that, since it was restored in the 19th century, has served as a display case for the affluent past of Bruges, which once was one of Europe's richest cities.

Tastefully furnished, the rooms of the Gruuthuse Museum are filled with treasures arranged to simulate the appearance of refined domestic interiors. There are windows inset with stained glass coats of arms; hand-carved beams; partition walls serving as backdrops for splendid pieces of furniture, as well as for tapestries, ceramics and items in precious metals (right). Dated 1520, this polychrome terracotta portrait of the young Charles V greets visitors at the entrance (opposite, far left).

with the privileged canon – Van Eyck created an image that also epitomizes a particular, and to the people of Bruges, extremely important kind of accomplishment – that of handling noble, costly materials with flawless skill. An entire culture can be seen to reside in this compelling marriage of substance and form, exquisite materials and masterful workmanship.

There is no doubt that Van Eyck depicted the materialism of pre-Renaissance Bruge more realistically elsewhere. His *Arnolfini Wedding Portrait*, for example, which hangs in the National Gallery in London, portrays a young Bruges couple of Italian origin standing together in an opulently furnished contemporary domestic interior. But the richness displayed in the London painting is decidedly that of well-to-do merchants or bankers, not saints and prelates. It does not possess the aristocratic refinement of the Groeninge work and of another Bruges masterpiece, Hans Memling's 1479 *Mystic Marriage of St. Catherine*, which is displayed in the chapel of St. John's Hospital. As in Van Eyck's *Madonna and Child*, the magnificence of the fabrics and decor in the Memling betray more than just a visual interest in material splendor. They suggest an engrained fascination for luxury.

The people of Bruges have a cultivated eye for fine materials and an instinct for knowing how to bring out the best in them. This gift for transforming raw materials could only result in the high quality that is the hallmark of everything that is produced in Bruges. It was also the impetus behind the city's early involvement in the most exacting facet of jewelery-making: diamond-cutting. Subsequently taken over by Antwerp, which has maintained its preeminence

In this touching reconstruction of an old-fashioned schoolroom, with its neat rows of terraced desks, you can almost hear the buzz of an impertinent fly distracting children from their lessons.

ever since, this specialty was developed in Bruges starting in the 14th century under the Burgundian Dukes. It symbolizes better than all other achievements of Bruges, the powerful alchemy of local craftsmanship. Although the citizens of Bruges did not transmute lead into gold, they knew how to change carbon into light. Their pioneering inventiveness gave diamonds, which were then imported raw from India via Genoa and Venice, their northern European brilliance and unchallenged supremacy among gems.

The people of Bruges are also known for their discriminating taste in *objects.* Just beside the Groeninge Museum, the Gruuthuse Museum provides an opportunity to assess this vaunted reputation. The mansion in which it is housed was falling into ruin when it was bought by the city in 1875. Its restoration was entrusted to the Bruges architect Louis Delacenserie, who assiduously returned the structure to a semblance of its original Gothic grandeur.

Today its galleries, fragrant with wood polish and waxed oak, present fine examples of rich furnishings from the past. Ceremonial silver and its everyday equivalent, ceramics from Delft and Moustiers, beautifully crafted musical instruments such as hurdy-gurdies, spinets, and harpsicords, as well as rare tools and utensils attest to the informed taste that predominated among Bruges' well-to-do families. Renaissance and Neo-classical cupboards, chests and other furniture pieces, as well as splendid tapestries – a few of which bear the Gothic "B" of Bruges – convey an idea of the comforts of home that were enjoyed day-to-day by the city's privileged many.

Many visitors form their opinions of Bruges interiors from the decor of the city's hotels. It should be noted that these establishments have improved

The Folklore Museum in the heart of the St. Anne neighborhood should not be missed. Its evocative, realistically detailed recreations of diverse work places from the past include the classroom shown here (left), a pharmacy and a hatmaker's shop, and feature the tools and other implements that were peculiar to each. While the utensils displayed in the 19th-century kitchen (opposite, left) may seem familiar enough, at least some of the accessories in the grocery store (opposite, lower right) and most of those in the cooper's workshop (opposite, upper right) are "new" to most visitors. The entrance to the Guildhall of the Archers of St. Sebastian is at number 178 Carmersstraat, in the eastern-most part of the city (pages 92 and 93).

ZAND
SODA
ZEEP

POE
EN
ZAE

greatly over the past 15 years with the aim, now accomplished, of providing the West Flanders capital with a hotel industry worthy of its status as a major tourist destination. Several of the bigger hotels that have recently been renovated have had their interiors refurbished by some of the region's top young decorators. While a unique hotel like *Die Swaene* may be reluctant to make the slightest change in its enduring neo-Gothic decor, others such as the Tuilerieen, on the Dijver, and its sister institution L'Orangerie, as well as the *Oud Huis Amsterdam* and the more contemporary *Montanus* have added overstuffed chairs, deep sofas, luminous paintings and, in cold weather, crackling fires to their amenities. Bruges' gradual transformation from a tourist attraction to a destination for discriminating travelers is thus comfortably underway.

The Guild of the Archers of St. Sebastian has occupied the same building for more than four centuries. Portraits of members and benefactors hang in the main hall, where a wide array of memorabilia, including a collection of bombards, is also displayed. The stained glass coats of arms in the windows recall guild members' participation in the Crusades (upper left); the black and white urns on the conference room table are still used for the election of new members (opposite). The harmonious color scheme and pleasing decor of the dining room in the Tuilerieen Hotel were chosen by Pieter Porters (pages 96 and 97).

Originally known by the name Van Brugghe, literally "Dupont" in French and akin to "Smith" in English, the Gruuthuse family made their fortune as brewers in the Middle Ages. Their name change was inspired by a commercial coup: they secured a monopoly on gruut, a mixture of flowers and herbs that was used, as hops are nowadays, to alleviate the bitterness of beer made from wheat and barley.

Today beer brewing in Bruges is largely ceremonial, but its various stages can still be witnessed at the *Straffe Hendrik* museum, which conducts tours and tastings. The famous *Gouden*

DEN EED
St SEBASTIAEN,
HOOFDMAN

Eggs as you like

Boom pub, which has been a fixture on Langestraat since 1587, offers several types of barrel beers, among them the delicious Brugse Tripel.

Knowledge of the pubs, taverns, brasseries, cafes and *kroegen* of Bruges (all these classifications, and more, are currently in use) can't be learned from books. These institutions, many of which serve local specialties like shrimp croquettes, are also lively centres of conversation and activity. In effect, they are purveyors and perpetuaters of a fine art of living. Some of them occupy historic sites: near St. Savior's Church, the *Cafedraal* shelters within the old city walls, which date from 1468 and once sheltered Erasmus himself. *Kroegen* are cafes that specialize in *witteke*, literally a "little white drink" of ginever, a potent alcohol whose subtle nuances are extolled by connoisseurs and mostly lost on amateurs. Another one of Bruges' cultivated tastes.

The cozy foyer (right) of the Tuilerieen Hotel on the Dijver gives an idea of the warm ambience of that reigns in all the rooms of this establishment. A note authenticity can be found in its small square window panes, many of which are the Venetian glass originals (above).

All of the old taverns take pride in their history. *De Garre*, nestled between the Markt and Burg squares, has a rather mysterious aura. Vlissinghe, which opened in 1515, is the most senior of them all. Its picturesque atmosphere seems to roll back the centuries.

In the same vicinity and to similar effect, the Folklore Museum evokes aspects of daily life in long-ago Bruges with truly life-like recreations of a pharmacy, a hat-makers shop, a cooper's workshop and a school room. These and several other period

The bar at the Tuilerieen, with its crackling fire and comfortable furnishings of leather and polished wood (left), is a relaxing place for a nightcap before ascending the wide, curving staircase (above) that leads to the guest rooms.

Known for its calm, elegance and authenticity, the Oud Huis Amsterdam on Spiegelrei reproduces the gentility of the fine art of living of the past.

establishments are set up in a string of houses formerly owned by the shoemakers' guild. Anything but petrified, the environment seems uncannily alive, with authentic old tools and other implements both carefully arranged and strewn about, as if their users' have just left for a quick lunch break. You probably won't find them talking shop over delicacies in the museum's *Zwarte Kat* (Black Cat) cafe, but visitors who take refreshment there are guaranteed an extension of their journey into the past.

Flemish cuisine is another one of the quotidian pleasures that are rife in Bruges. Here, rabbit and hare are cooked in beer; fowl is the star ingredient in *waterzooi*, which is prepared with flavorful buillon and cream; red meats are steamed and then stewed in *carbonnades*; eel is served *au vert*, with a watercress, cervil and tarragon sauce. To gourmets all over Europe, the name "Bruges" is indissociable from "*pralines*" (hand-made chocolates with an array of scrumptious fillings) and a whole host of specialty sweets that include caramel "babeluttes" and raspberry-flavored cones called "cuberdons."

So tantalizingly evoked in the paintings of Frans Snyders, the pleasures of the palate contribute no small share to the Flemish atmosphere of abundance. The gastronomic centre of Bruges is the Vismarkt (fish market), where today as in ages past, sole and turbot, staples of the local *haute cuisine*, as well as the humble herring and gray shrimp change hands

To get an even better idea of the fine art of living specific to West Flanders, visitors may wish to stay in one of the region's many private guest houses. At Number 11 on Groenerei, the living room, with its lovely light-toned woodwork (left), and the charming garden (above) afford unequaled comfort and privacy.

in an atmosphere of unmitigated exuberance. Fortunately, the ebullient mood is not dampened by the severity of the architecture that houses it. Inaugurated in 1821, the Neo-classical building with its strictly aligned Doric columns presents a cold contrast to the lively activity it encloses and to the romantic gabled roofs of its neighbors. However, the stiffness and incongruity that appear so salient at market time evaporate after hours, giving way to a poise and nobility that surely would be missed if the structure were to change or disappear.

Beautiful wood paneling, exquisite fabrics, and furniture and objects that reflect personal rather than institutional taste make the reception room of the Romantik Pandhotel an ideal spot for a fireside game of chess (right).

Another kind of nobility resides in Bruges' sumptuous lacework, some rare pieces of which date back to the 15th century. Both the Gruuthuse and Arentshuis museums have fine collections containing some sublime examples. These institutions, and not souvenir shop windows, are fitting showcases for the most exquisitely crafted works the city has ever produced. Although lace-making originated in Venice, it reached its technical and artistic apogee in Flanders, and specifically in Bruges.

By some sort of cruel irony, this luxury item *par excellence* was confected by women who, when not impoverished, were of modest means. Wives of laborers or fishermen, they worked to supplement their husbands' meager incomes and often ruined their eyesight in the process of creating goods that would give visual pleasure to people more privileged

The walls and interior spaces of the Montanus Hotel date back to the 17th century, but its decor is resolutely contemporary – and most unusual for Bruges. The salon's light, harmonious color scheme is offset by off-white slipcovers and curtains (right). In the dining room (above), built-in serving counters, rattan chairs, large contemporary paintings and designer vases and accessories contribute to a clean, modern look. The guest rooms in this charming hotel near the beguinage are as casual and welcoming as the guest rooms in a family house (above right). Even the garden is designed along contemporary lines. It shelters a wood-framed bungalow, also for guests, with a Scandinavian accent (pages 104 and 105).

19

Near the Groeninge Museum, the elegant Den Dijver restaurant is a gracious setting for sampling some of Bruges' traditional dishes (above). The menu includes a variety of foods prepared with beer as well as salmon cooked "a la Sixtus," a regional specialty.

than themselves. Their art demanded keen vision, rapt attention, unfailing dexterity and years of training. The famous *point de fee*, said to have been inspired by the webs of tiny spiders, required the use of 600 bobbins at a time.

Extremely rare, old and now priceless are the pieces composed of several large swathes of lace stitched together end to end. It would not be too much to say that these compound works unite the labor of several lifetimes. Compared to these chefs-d'oeuvre, the doilies mass-produced in the Far East and sold everywhere today as lace are not deserving of the name. Crowded into shop window displays all over Bruges, they pay paltry homage to one of the city's finest arts.

With the invention of the Jacquard loom and the entry of women into the paid workforce, lacemaking declined in Bruges until by the 1970s it was pursued by only a determined, unenvied few. Curious passersby could still admire the skills of these seasoned women working busily, and as always, in the open doorways of their homes around the Walplein. It was clear that they were practicing a fast-disappearing art. In an attempt to prevent it from vanishing altogether, a lacemaking academy was established in the St. Anne neighborhood, where it continues successfully to perpetuate the knowledge and the endlessly repeated gestures of generations of anonymous artists.

Proud of their customs and traditions and conscious of the allure that these hold for tourists, the people of Bruges, like their British neighbors, are only too happy to reenact historic moments and events. Unrivaled in this respect are the armed guilds, Bruges' ancient militia, which are now run like private

The kitchen of Den Gouden Harynck, near the Church of Our Lady, pays culinary tribute to the fishmonger's shop that preceded it on this site (above). Other restaurants known for their settings are the Ducs de Bourgogne (below right), De Bekoring (below left) and the Egmond (above right).

The refreshing Blanche de Bruges and the heady Bourgogne de Flandres are just two of the dozens of regional beers offered in local pubs. These amber brews are traditional accompaniments to a meal of mussels harvested in the environs. In many brasseries, such as the Cafe de Arts, coffee is served in shiny copper pitchers (left). The Vlissinghe cafe's picturesque decor and excellent service have assured customer satisfaction at this, Bruges' oldest tavern, since time immemorial. The only feature that has needed altering are the gas lamps, which now use electricity.

* lasagna 850,-
* lasagna verde
650,-
* pompoensoep
101,-

The huge variety and superb quality of the shellfish and fish, both smoked and fresh, that are sold daily at the fishmarket tend to distract attention from the stately Neo-classical design of the market building itself, which looks somewhat out of place in its medieval surroundings.

clubs: the guilds of the Archers of St. Sebastian and of the Crossbowmen of St. George. From Carmersstraat, the guild-house of the former can be distinguished by its hexagonal brick tower. At the entrance, the coat of arms of Jerusalem brought back from the Holy Land serves as a proud reminder that its members fought in the Crusades. Tradition has it that all British sovereigns have been honorary members since the 17th century, when Charles II, then exiled in Bruges, became an enthusiastic habitue of the guild. As for the Crossbowmen of the Guild of St. George, they still observe customs that were instituted when the association was founded in 1321. Twice a week, members aim their sights at feathered targets that are hoisted 36 meters in the air on bizarre poles especially designed for the purpose. Still, the emphasis of the meetings is less on sports than on reinforcing the age-old bonds of Flemish solidarity.

Despite their fondness for anachronisms, it would be a mistake to take the people of Bruges for backward-looking sentimentalists gripped by nostalgia for the past. Quite to the contrary, they are eager to be recognized for their contemporary achievements. The wistfulness really belongs to the city's visitors, who take delight in faded treasures and in soaking up the ambience of retro tea houses with nary a thought to the nearby manufacturers of locomotives and farm machinery or to the exploits of the world-class football team FC Bruges. The two sides of Bruges' coin are truly opposite: one is old-fashioned and seductive; the other modern but rather humdrum.

Sweets of every kind are another Bruges specialty. Shop windows are crammed with hand-made chocolates (Van Oost's are shown on the left), biscuits made with cumin, cinnamon and other spices, cone-shaped raspberry confections called "cuberdons" and caramels dubbed "babeluttes" (above).

Every bit of the dynamism and prestige generated by a major cultural event such as 2002 is needed to recast the image of Bruges to fit its modern identity. Time will tell whether or not the public is prepared to accept the change, but the city itself seems already to be benefiting from the breath of fresh air that is sweeping in with the contemporary projects and performances it is hosting. Bruges' ever increasing population of resident artists are encouraged by what they see as the emergence of a progressive cultural climate that is finally worthy of the city. It seems that the old lion of Flanders, the *Vlaamse Leeuw*, is getting ready to roar once again.

Among the masses of machine-made laces imported from the Far East, it is still possible to find in certain boutiques examples of the antique bobbin lace that for centuries gave Bruges' an international reputation as a city of sublime refinement.

Collectors with an eye for the off-beat do well to visit Pol Standaert's attic, which is stuffed to the gills with plaster molds and stucco objects that his family business has been producing for several generations. Appointments can be arranged in his shop on Witte Leertouwerstraat, not far from Groenerei.

Seaward

SEAWARD

The sun at close of day
Clothes the fields of hay,
Then the canals, at last the town entire
In hyacinth and gold.

The Bruges paradox, a reference to the city's dilemma of having the sea within view but impractically out of reach, presents certain advantages to hikers and explorers. Most notably, it provides them the pleasure of discovering an intermediary zone – the luminous, breezy polders, which are traversed by canals and punctuated by dikes. Nothing could be more natural than extending a visit to the city out into these lowlands between Bruges and the sea. As thoroughly shaped by human effort as the urban environment itself, their serene landscape comprises a vegetal, perennially verdant pendant to the mineral concatenation of bricks, stones and tiles farther inland.

Here too, cars are anathema to the attentive traveler. The best way to approach the Zwin and the coast beyond it is to leave Bruge via the old Reie waterway and forge ahead along the Damsevaart, a channel that follows the commercial shipping route of the Middle Ages. This leads to the village of Damme. Some people choose to go up the canal aboard the *Lamme Goedzak*, whose fake paddle wheel adds a tacky note to the otherwise picturesque environment. Others prefer to bike or walk along the towpath. Covering the

It's hard to imagine that this lazy canal between Bruges and Damme was once a vital commercial route bustling with activity and excitement (pages 114 and 115). That was before the Zwin silted up, inexorably blocking maritime traffic. Today, the old windmill, a few white houses and a procession of bullrushes, willows and poplars insure the site's Bruegelian charm (left and above). In warm weather, a paddle-wheeler ripples the languid waters.

Formerly the outer harbor of Bruges, Damme today is landlocked. The dense network of channels and canals that guaranteed its past affluence now functions mainly to drain the polders and reflect the changeable Flemish sky.

The Zwin is admirably deserving of its reputation as a tranquil, well-preserved environment. Its fastidiously preserved towpaths are now the domain of hikers and strollers who may encounter a few pretty dwellings and old farms, nothing more, along their way (opposite). A kind of ultimate focal point, the spire of Damme's Church of Our Lady can be seen through the fog settling in over the canal banks (below).

total distance of about seven kilometers affords just enough time to ponder the dramatic consequences of a violent storm that hit this spot in 1134. The winds were so high and the tides so strong that they carved out an inlet, the famous Zwin channel, that wended its way to within a few cable-lengths of Bruges. The locals saw it as a gift from God, and they wasted no time in building a sea wall, thereby creating the site of Damme.

On the way to Sluis, the Damme canal changes course at the site known as The Siphon (opposite). A certain Baron Serret built himself this mansion, called Le Chateau des Trois Rois (Three Kings' Castle), near Beernem in 1802. Although some of the stones used in the building's construction are from the old Church of St. Donatian, there is little Flemish about its architecture.

Less than 50 years later, after it had become a busy fishing village and prosperous outer port, Damme was given the statutory rights of a city by Philip of Alsace, the Count of Flanders. This entitled Damme to reap the financial benefits of its providentially strategic geographical position: at that time it was both the port of entry and obligatory staging post for all boats going to and departing from Bruges. Within a few decades, Damme had grown rich from the taxes it collected on the ceaseless flow of maritime traffic.

Signs of the town's prosperity proliferated, but it was only after the village was sacked in 1213 by the forces of the French King Philippe Auguste that the people of Damme began to think big, and pompous. Ostentatious residences sprang up along the branching village roads. Like their neighbours in Bruges, the citizens of Damme wanted a town hall, a Gothic church, a hospital and a beguinage. And like Bruges, Damme instituted guilds and issued commercial trading licences. It held a monopoly on wines imported from southwest France, the forebears of today's Bordeaux, and on herring brought in from Sweden. The village's Herring Market, which today looks poignantly forlorn, contains the memory of the days in the mid-15th century when 28

Planted to reinforce the canal banks and buttress the dikes, rows of diligently tended trees festoon the Zwin region. Around Damme, willows and giant poplars can be seen from afar lining the waterways with verdant curtains that can reach up to 20 meters in height and tilt in the direction of the prevailing wind.

million herring changed hands in Damme

There seemed to be no limit to the town's prospects for expansion when, early in the 14th century, the Zwin silted up, putting an end to the economic boom. The population was reluctant to admit defeat, however, and, ignoring the evidence, they continued to pour money into prestigious projects. The new town hall, a powerful Gothic structure, wasn't yet completed when, in 1468 Damme proudly staged the lavish wedding of Charles the Bold and Margaret of York, which was presided over by the Bishop of Salisbury. St. John, as the house is called where the marriage festivities were celebrated, and its neighbors *De Grote Sterre* (the Big Star) and *Craynest* (Crow's Nest), still possess an insistent splendor that now looks bizarrely out of place in this country village.

The St. Jacques farm near Hoeke (above), at the crossroad taken in earlier times by pilgrims heading for Santiago de Campostela, was recently tastefully restored. A fine example of the regional style known as Scaldian Gothic, the 15th-century tower of the Church of Our Lady (opposite) in Damme rises 45 meters above the surrounding countryside.

Reclaimed from the sea with patience and determination, the low-lying polders, rich with thick green grasses that grow all year 'round, are devoted to grazing (below). White-washed farms with red-tiled roofs appear like grace notes in the emerald pastures (right).

Tirelessly, Damme modeled itself on its powerful neighbor, whose own affluence and opulent style were already *passe*. Damme was such a succesful mimic that it became a kind of small-scale Bruges. Unfortunately its diminutive size provided no insurance against major disaster, and its economic ruin proved to be even more brutal than the one suffered by Bruges.

Thus the wheel of fortune turns. If Damme has a place in today's collective memory, it is as the home of Tyl Ulenspiegel, the allegorical character invented in 1867 by Charles De Coster, a Flemish novelist who wrote in French, as was costumary in his time. Many Belgians know the first lines of his

As the obligatory staging area for goods bound for Bruges, Damme benefited from the dynamism of its powerful neighbor. Like Bruges, Damme desired the prestigious trappings of a prosperous community: a town hall, a monumental church, a hospital, a beguinage and stately homes. The remains of its former pretensions can still be found, but beyond the lively main square and the Kerkstraat in the centre of Damme, the little lanes and deserted squares are pervaded by a small-village serenity .

Now beguilingly rural, the Herring Market Square holds the memory of the long-ago time when Damme rivaled Ostend in the herring trade. The fish were then stocked in barrels, much to the profit and delight of the coopers' guild.

picaresque work *The Legend of Ulenspiegel* by heart: "When May was unfolding the hawthorn blossom, Ulenspiegel, son of Claes, was born in Damme." The celebrated protagonist – clever, heroic, engaging and endearing – has become an emblem of the Flemish resistance to the Spanish Occupation and Inquisition. Several films have been made that are based on the book: Gerard Philipe plays the lead role in the French one, and there is a fine Russian production. It is not surprising that Tyl's native village has avidly embraced him as a mascot. It has erected a statue of him and gladly caters to tourists following his trail.

Beautiful wrought-iron signs announce that Damme has been transformed into a "Village of Books" (top below). The restaurant, 'Le Siphon,' that has borne the same name in the village for decades, knows how to refresh the weary hiker (under below).

The squared-off tower of the Church of Our Lady in Damme seems to surge up between these straight-lined gables (above). The outsized mass of the city hall, designed as a simplified version of its model in Bruges and built between 1464 and 1469, hovers over the houses at the entrance to the village on the far side of the lock (opposite).

The proximity of a major attraction such as Bruges does not necessarily benefit tourism in the surrounding region. Most visitors to Bruges never venture beyond the walls of the old city or think to inquire what lies on the other side. Only a few well-informed, adventurous spirits with time to spare bother to explore the polders and the area known as the Zwin – and that is part of the region's charm. The unspoiled beauty of the landscape and the quaint charm of its dwellings are irresistibly appealing, as local property agents are finding out, to an elite group of Belgian artists searching for second homes or remote get-aways. An inspiring breeze seems to blow over the polders. It was surely with these new residents and their guests in mind that in 1997 Damme assumed a new vocation: that of a "Village of Books." An influx of book shops and a flurry of readings and other literary events have conferred an intellectual accent that is neither ponderous nor unwelcome at this long-ago birthplace of the great medieval poet Jacob van Maerlant.

P
300m
Taverne

At the Eethuis de Zuidkant, in an atmosphere steeped in charm, variety and freshness are the order of each day. Committed chefs Lynn and Christophe let the seasons determine their menus.

Water, of course, is the polders' dominant element and principal asset. Omnipresent, it creates the haunting, misty atmosphere that so often pervades the region. The multitude of dikes, locks, siphons and canals testify to man's mastery of water and clay, the sole means by which this land, which was originally unsuited to human habitation, could have been domesticated. Damme itself had to endure the digging of the canal that runs between Bruges and Sluis. The project was part of Napolean's scheme to link Antwerp to Dunkerque, and thereby circumvent the blockade of the Continental System. The first section – between Bruges and Damme – was dug by Spanish prisoners of war. The Dutch continued the channel all the way to Sluis.

Because of its orientation, this is the first of all the canals to freeze in winter – a fact well known by local skaters, who rush to the ice as soon as it is solid. For miles on end, the colorful processions of gliding, sliding, twirling figures as well as those clustered around makeshift stands selling hot wine, call to mind the winter scenes of Hendrik Avercamp and Pieter Bruegel the Younger. The burly, joyful silhouettes depicted in the 17th century seem miraculously to have reappeared in the 21st. The afternoons often conclude with the most energetic of the merry-makers skating across the border into Holland and pushing on as far as Sluis. There they buy necklaces composed of small rolls of bread – a specialty of the town – and wear them proudly back to Bruges as trophies, and proof of their stamina.

Another attraction of the Zwin region is its unique and abundant flora and fauna. Birds in particular thrive in the wet, wooded habitat. Professional

On the same street, Den Heerd restaurant serves regional specialities such as eel "au vert" in a pastel interior designed by decorator Philip Simoen (above). De Stamper farm is discreetly ensconced near Lapscheure, on the outskirts of Damme (pages 132 and 133).

ornithologists and amateur bird-watchers alike flock to the marshy Romboustwerve nature reserve, which is thick with reeds and bullrushes, to espy red-crested pochards, wigeons, greylag geese, egrets, moorhens, spoonbills, ruffs, avocets, oyster-catchers, gray herons and white storks – among other types of feathered denizens. Trees are something else again: few varieties can survive in such conditions. The crack willow, whose silhouette would make a fitting emblem for the region, is one of them. Poplars are another. These tall trees lining the edges of dams consume such enormous quantities of water that, like natural pumps, they help dry out the land.

It is important to keep in mind the fact that the polders were once *schorre*, or flats, which were inundated at high tide. For a long time, sheep grazing was the sole activity these salt-soaked lands

With its sumptuous willow-lined drive and its unusual (for the region) mansard roof and blue shutters hanging against white-washed walls, De Stamper has retained the rusticity of its 17th-century origins (above). Marc Nyssen, descendent of a long line of farmers and a farmer himself, has turned his charming home into a much admired inn.

Comfortable guest rooms have been created under the eaves, and antique utensils that have been relieved of their functional duties decorate the entrance (left and above).

Forty guests can sit comfortably around the two large tables in the dining room, which is heated by an impressive wood-burning stove.

would support. Flanders' spinning and weaving industries stem from this very place. The scarce higher ground provided the only arable soil. Still today, these knolls and hillocks are reserved for cereal crops, while the lowlands are used for raising livestock. Herds have varied over the years: today's pastures are filled with peaceful cows, whose lazy ways harmonize with the spirit of the site.

It took centuries for the local farmers to build the curving dikes that still protect this land from encroachment by the sea. In fact, the polders constitute one the most radical transformations of the natural world that has ever been wrought by human hands. The titanic project could never have been accomplished without the energetic participation of the monastic communities that pitched in and adopted it as their own. Members of the Cistercian order in particular played a key role in the work of "polderization." Those affiliated to the Abbey of the Coxyde Dunes were able to charge enormous rents for the land which they had rendered arable. The huge tithe barn at Ter Doest, near Lissewege, which served as the storage depot for these payments in kind from farmers who cultivated the newly fertile fields, gives an idea of their magnitude. Monumental, it is one of the oldest non-religious buildings still in use in Europe. Even more extraordinary is the fact that, since its construction in the 12th century, it has never changed function: today as always, it stores the harvest.

Except for its famous barn, all that remains of Ter Doest Abbey, a dependency of the Abbey of the Coxyde Dunes, are a 17th-century monastic building that has been converted into a restaurant (opposite and left) and a tiny Baroque chapel (above).

Built by Cistercian monks, Ter Doest's 12th-century tithe barn is a veritable secular cathedral. The roof alone is a tour de force. In continuous use since it was completed, this is one of the few rural buildings in all of Europe that is more than seven hundred years old (right). The charm of Blankenberge is greatly enhanced by its jetty-esplanades (pages 140 and 141).

The barn's gigantic roof is supported by strong square beams that look as solid as stone. No tree native to the area could have furnished such a trunk: the one that did was floated down from Scandinavia. Legend has it that by the time the giant tree arrived it was so thoroughly impregnated with salt that, after it had dried, a superhuman effort was required to drive nails into it.

Nearby, in Lissewege, charming white-washed fishermen's houses seem incalculably remote from the huge industrial port that lies just a short distance away. The bell tower of the village church is curiously flat-roofed – but not for the reasons one might seek in the religious strife that pitted Protestants against Roman Catholics in the 16th century. Rather, local bell towers also functioned as light houses: they were purposely truncated so that fires could be built on their summits to guide passing ships. This is proof, if such is needed, that the coast is close, and the sea ever-present in the hearts and minds of the people of the region.

The wide Baudouin Canal, which was built at the turn of the 20th century with the aim of connecting landlocked Bruges to the new port at Zeebrugge, is the city's industrialized trade link with the modern world. Docks line its banks for miles, and, as in all big ports, a chaos of cranes, railroad tracks, warehouses and silos spreads out in all directions.

Strange as it may seem, this clamorous complex is flanked by elegant beach resorts that were the haunts of the rich, chic and aristocratic in the 19th century: Knokke-le-Zoute on the northeast, and Blankenberge on the

southwest. The latter's strand used to be visible on clear days from the top of the belfry in Bruges. Between the First and Second World Wars, a long dike that doubles as an esplanade, locally referred to as an "estacade," was built out from the shoreline. Perhaps inevitably, the structure calls to mind its famous counterpart in Brighton. There is nothing quite so exhilarating as walking there in the salty breeze, in a golden light, between fleecy sea and foamy sky....

Out there, just beyond the horizon, due west, is England. Looking out from this vantage point, one is inclined to see things the way Jacques Brel did:

...T'was the north wind that rent the land
Between Zeebrugge and England.
London's not like it was before the deluge
The tip of Bruges acting so grand.
London's now just a suburb of Bruges
Lost at sea....

The Oesterput Devriendt restaurant is situated inside the fish exchange just behind the port (above). Looking out to sea, who could tell that Bruges lies just a few miles inland (opposite and pages 144 and 145)?

USEFUL ADDRESSES

This list was drawn up with the aim of reflecting the city of charm and refinement that is described in the main text. The hotels, guest houses, restaurants and shops that have been selected for inclusion are those that, in the editors' opinions, best represent that spirit.

Unless otherwise indicated, the establishments are listed alphabetically in each section.

Page numbers that appear in parentheses refer to illustrations.

When telephoning Bruges from abroad, dial the Belgian country code, 32, before the local number. From elsewhere in Belgium, first dial 0.

HOTELS

ADORNES
Sint Annarei, 26
Tel. 50.34.13.36
Situated on one of the city's quietest and most elegant canals, this twenty-room hotel, simple and comfortable, occupies three adjoining 17th-century houses. A gracious local touch: guests are given the use of bicycles, free of charge.

EGMOND
Minnewater, 15
Tel. 50 34 14 45
(p. 20-21)
This ultra-romantic hotel has just eight rooms. Its setting is a charming 19th-century house.

MONTANUS
Nieuwe Gentweg, 78
Tel. 50 33 11 76
(p. 103 and pp. 104-105)
The walls of this lovely hotel date from the 17th century but its decor is resolutely modern. Suites 17 and 18, which are adjacent to one of the city' most beautiful almshouses, are stunning. We confess a preference for the rooms in the 1930s-style annex as well as for the contemporary chic of number 19 in the garden bungalow.

DE ORANGERIE
Kartuizerinnenstraat, 10
Tel. 50 34 16 49
The very talented sister of the proprietor of the famous Tuilerieen hotel has created this attractive establishment in a charming house overlooking the Dijver.

OUD HUIS AMSTERDAM
Spiegelrei, 3
Tel. 50 34 14 45
(p. 100)
Set within a row of four 17th-century town houses near Jan Van Eyckplein, this is one of Bruges' most pleasant hotels. The traditional decor of the bar and reception rooms is exquisite and warmed by open fires in chilly weather. Among other choice guest rooms: number 27 overlooks the garden and has exposed beams; number 33 is smaller but delightful; 44, a suite overlooking the canal, is quite grandiose.

ROMANTIK PANDHOTEL
Pandreitje, 16
Tel. 50 34 06 66
(p. 102)
Despite its close proximity to the fish market, the little square where this comfortable hotel is located is an oasis of calm. It occupies an 18th-century house whose interior has been all but transformed: only the original light-toned woodwork remains in the common spaces, notably in the living room and dining room, which contains a big Aga stove from England. Some of the guest rooms are done up Ralph-Lauren-style. Another plus: the hotel's owner knows Bruges inside-out and is an infallible source of good addresses.

DE SWAENE
Steenhouwerdijk, 1
Tel. 50 34 27 98
Thanks to its fabulous site and international renown, this grand hotel continues to attract a steady stream of sophisticated travelers. It should be noted, however, that the Neo-gothic decor has not yet been refurbished with the same thoroughness that has transformed many of the city's other hotels into truly charming establishments.

TER DUINEN
Langerei, 52
Tel. 50 33 04 37
Modest but very well maintained, this small hotel is located on the canal in a lovely, quiet neighborhood. The garden boasts a charming, authentic tea pavilion.

DE TUILERIEEN
Dijver, 7
Tel. 50 34 36 91
(pp. 96 to 99)
Its excellent position on the Dijver canal, a stone's throw from the Groeninge Museum, is just one of the strong points of this beautiful hotel, which is housed in a heavily restored 17th-century building. An indoor swimming pool is another, and the rather audacious decor by Flemish designer Pieter Porters yet another. The soft palette and pretty lighting in the dining room make any meal there divine; and the bar with its fireplace and view of the canal is an ideal spot for a refreshing break during the course of a busy day.

GUESTHOUSES

As everwhere in Belgium, Bruges teems with guest houses. The following have been selected for their charm.

NUMBER 11
Peerdenstraat, 11
Tel. 50 33 06 75
(p. 101)
The approach to this well-kept 17th-century house – a romantic little bridge across the Groenerei canal – is in itself enchanting. Once inside, the living room, with its pleasant light-wood panelling, is a restful place to relax. We recommend the suite that opens onto the enclosed garden. The walls are lined with bookshelves and outside there's a covered terrace – an ideal

breakfast spot in warm weather.

'T GEERWIJN
Chris De Loof
Geerwijnstraat, 14
Tel. 50 34 05 44
A pleasant bed and breakfast in a pair of 19th-century brick houses with stepped gables.

PAUL & ROOS GHEERAERT-VANDEVELDE
Riddersstraat, 9
Tel. 50 33 56 27
He is an architect, she is a painting restorer, and together they extend a warm welcome to guests in their 1856 townhouse, which is midway between the Burg and the St. Anne quarter.

CLASSICS
Carmersstraat, 16
Tel. 50 34 17 35
Concert pianist Hanna Jaszyk welcomes guests into her peaceful corner house near the Church of Jerusalem. The decor is central European, and the regional dishes prepared by the proprietor, delicious.

BED & BRUGES
Louise and Francis Hardy
Annuntiatenstraat, 105
Tel. 50 34 43 38
A contemporary-style house built in 1997 in a quiet garden.

IN THE VICINITY...

DE STAMPER
Marc Nyssen
Zuiddijk, 12
8340 Damme
Tel. 50 50 01 97
(pp. 132 to 135)
Beware: the little road that leads to this lovely farm outside Damme is not easy to find, but that does not seem to discourage people from reaching it. The food and lodgings are so highly reputed that reservations are a must. The lively atmosphere of this working farm provides an added attraction.

HOLIDAY HOUSES IN DAMME
Huyse de Grote Sterre
Jacob van Maerlantstraat, 3
8340 Damme
Tel. 50 37 00 47
The tourist information centre in Damme provides up-to-date lists of vacation rentals.

RESTAURANTS AND TAVERNS

DE BEKORING
Arsenaalstraat, 53/55
Tel. 50 34 41 57
A tiny 17th-century house near the beguinage. Wood fire, regional cooking and dinner by candelight. One of the most romantic spots in Bruges.

'T BOURGOENSCHE CRUYCE
Wollestraat, 41
Tel. 50 33 79 26
Customers are mainly attracted by the splendid view through small-paned windows, but the gastronomy is satisfying too.

THE CAFEDRAAL
Zilverstraat, 38
Tel. 50 34 08 45
This lively tavern occupies a 15th-century house and garden in the shadow of the cathedral tower. Among its specialties are the famous tiny gray shrimp, which are eaten raw, and a huge array – like the kind found in Spain –of various types of ham.

DEN DIJVER
Dijver, 5
Tel. 50 33 60 69
(p. 106)
A beautiful site, elegant decor and kitchen celebrated for its beer-based preparations.

DEN GOUDEN HARYNCK
Groeninge, 25
tel. 50 33 76 37
(p. 107)
This pretty, low-ceilinged restaurant in the heart of the tourist district behind the Church of Our Lady specializes in seafood, although chef Philippe Serruys' *risotto aux petits legumes a la provencale* is the menu's star attraction. Reservations are recommended. We enjoyed the tables beside the garden.

DEN GOUDEN KORENHALM
Oude Oostendsesteenweg, 79a
Tel 50 31 33 93
Despite its location close to the centre of the city, this elegant restaurant's home seems like a country manor. In fine weather, children can romp in the garden while parents linger at table. The service is pleasant, the food savory, and the tasting menu well worth trying.

DE KARMELIET
Langestraat, 19
Tel. 50 33 82 59
Run by Chapel-trained chef Geert van Hecke, this is undoubtedly the finest restaurant in Bruges. People come from near and far to dine on French sea scallops with black truffles and ham or on sweet and savory biscuits with roast langoustines and to indulge in rarefied desserts such as warm ravioli filled with vanilla creme and garnished with cooked apple. Despite its three Michelin stars and upscale clientele, the establishment is modestly housed in an unpretentious brick house.

RAYMOND
Eiermarkt, 5
Tel. 50 33 78 48
A big, wanna-be Parisian brasserie on a lively street that bends behind the Markt has the advantage of not being hampered by the restricted serving hours and menus of its generic model. Shellfish and a wide range of local specialties are offered.

DE SNIPPE
Nieuwe Gentweg, 33
Tel. 50 33 70 70
Under the sign of the woodcock, Luc Huysentruit serves excellent fish dishes. Well, why not? Handsome frescoes adorn the walls.

DE VISSCHERIE
Vismarkt, 8
Tel. 50 33 02 12

CHURCHES
1 Church of Jerualem
2 Church of Our Lady
3 Cathedral of St. Savior

MUSEUM AND MONUMENTS
4 Groeninge Museum
5 Gruuthuse Museum
6 Memling Museum
7 Folklore Museum
8 Museum of Our Lady of the Potterei
9 City Hall
10 Beguinage
11 Guild of the Archers of St. Sebastian
12 Fish market

ALMSHOUSES
13 Meulenare
14 St. Joseph
15 de Vos

HOTELS, CAFES, RESTAURANTS
16 Tuilerieen Hotel
17 Montanus Hotel
18 Oud Huis Amsterdam Hotel
19 Number 11 guest house
20 Cafe Vlissinghe

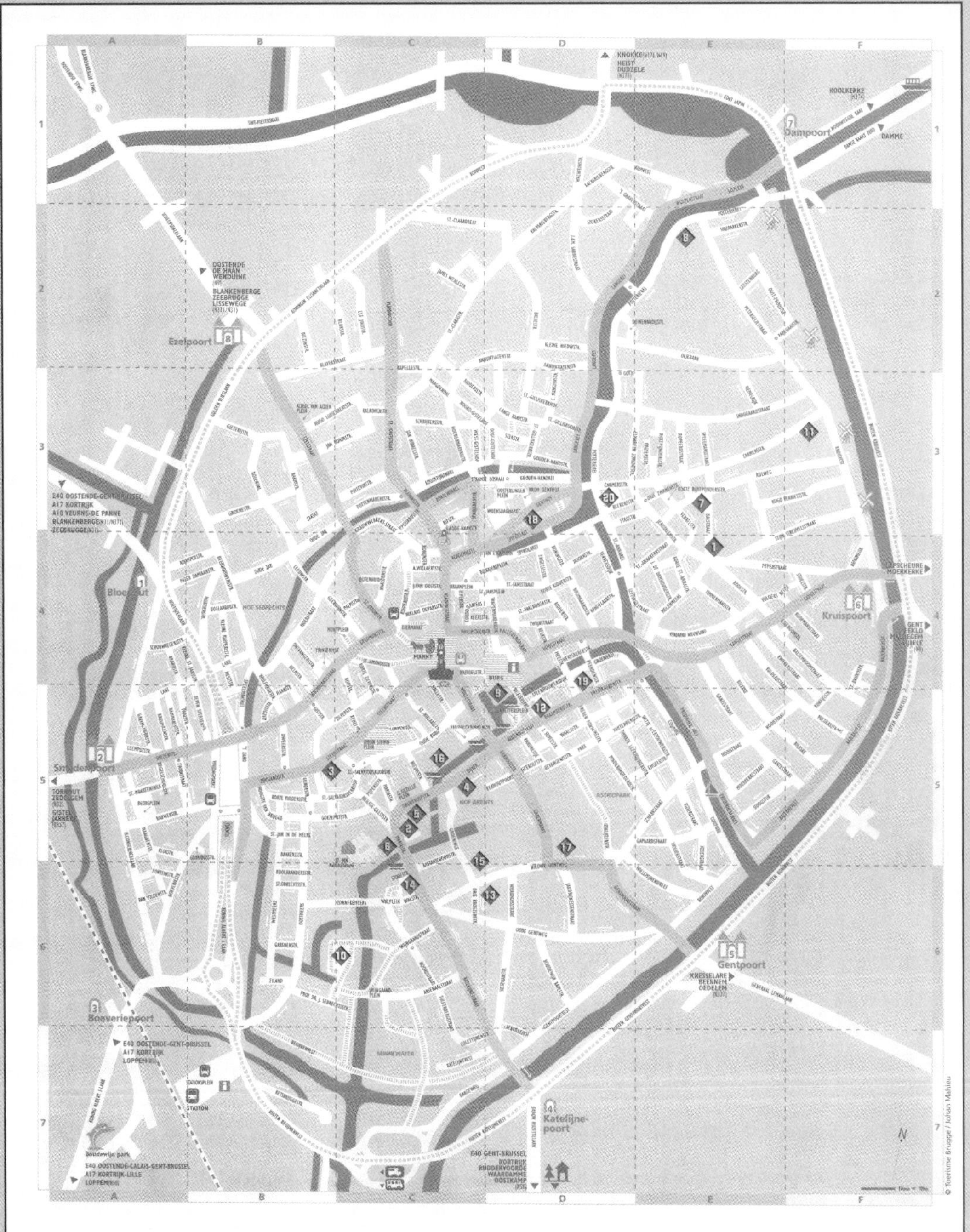

This elegant restaurant's contemporary decor belies its centuries-old structure, but its name which means, "the fishery," and location point, directly to the marvelous seafood on offer.

DE ZILVEREN PAUW
Zilverstraat, 41
Tel. 50 33 55 66
One of the star chefs of Bruges, Patrick Devos, is a familiar mustachioed, bespectacled face on the city's epicurean scene. In his Art Nouveau-style restaurant, he serves inventive contemporary fare with flair.
The tasting menu, with its six courses and five wines, is particularly tempting.

'T ZONNEKE
Genthof, 5
Tel. 50 33 07 81
The time-honoured specialties of this house, such as shrimp croquettes and eels *au vert*, never go out of style, nor does the charm of the architecture – dated 1507 – that frames it.

IN THE VICINITY

The restaurants are listed geographically, starting with the closest to the city.

DINE IN A HOTEL SCHOOL

HOEVE CORTVRIENDT
Oliebaan, 4
Tel. 50 33 52 19
Restaurant of the Spermalie school. Haute cuisine at low prices in a historic setting. There's just one hitch: customers must arrive between 12.15 and 12.30 pm or between 6 and 6.30 pm.

LA CASSEROLE
Groene Poortdreef, 17
8200 St. Michiels
Tel. 50 40 30 30
Listed in the *Michelin* guide, this establishment outside the city is a favorite among Bruges restaurant-goers. Filets of soles and medallions of venison are served in a rustic setting.

DEN HEERD
Jacob ven Maerlanstraat, 7
8340 Damme
Tel. 50 35 44 00
(p. 131)
The pleasing features of this small restaurant include a modern decor and welcoming fireplace.

EETHUIS DE ZUIDKANT
Jacob van Maerlanstraat, 6
8340 Damme
Tel. 50 37 16 76
(p. 130)
When asked to name the specialty of the house, the hostess replies, "Freshness." And it's true that her husband, the chef, is a stickler for impeccable ingredients. Lunch is served in the garden when the weather permits.

GOEDENDAG
Lisseweegs Vaartje, 2
8380 Lissewege
Tel. 50 54 53 35
An enjoyable stop in a lovely village.

HOF TER DOEST
Ter Doeststraat, 4
8380 Lissewege
Tel. 50 54 40 82
(pp. 136, 137 and 139)
The huge dining room may be impersonal and the fare unpretentious, but this establishment, which occupies a monastic building beside the abbey's illlustrious tithe barn, never disappoints travelers or regulars. Particularly busy on weekends.

SIPHON
Damsevaart Oost
8340 Oostkerke
Tel 50 62 02 02
The rustic decor and checked gingham tablecloths contribute to the pleasure of regional cooking copiously served. This restaurant is popular with everyone from locals to the royal family. Reservations required.

DE OESTERPUT
Oude Wenduinsesteenweg, 16
8370 Blankenberge
Tel. 50 41 10 35
(p. 142)

Situated in a corner of a large shed beside the fish exchange, this seafood restaurant is as close as one could wish to the source of its main culinary attraction.

CAFES AND TEA ROOMS

CAFE DES ARTS
Markt, 32
Tel. 50 33 34 68
(p. 108)
Like most of the cafes on the Markt, this one meets high standards. You can enjoy a meal or simply stop for coffee served in a pretty copper pitcher. Large Flemish landscape paintings decorate the walls.

(CAFES AND TEA ROOMS, CONT.)

DETAVERNIER
Wijngaardstraat, 8
Tel. 50 33 54 47
Pretty, old-fashioned tea room between Markt and the beguinage. Delicious waffles and other pastries, hot chocolate, the works....

DE GARRE
De Garre, 1
Tel. 50 34 10 29
Packed into two floors on a narrow passage between Markt and Burg, this cafe's interior looks like a scene from an old Flemish painting. It carries approximately one hundred brands of beer, and the courteous, efficient service enables customers virtually to eat on the fly.

DE PROVEVERIE
Katelijnestraat, 6
Tel. 50 33 08 87
This is the trendiest tea room in town, at least for the moment. Don't let its allure make you forget about visiting the lovely almshouse next door, though.

VLISSINGHE
Blekersstraat, 2
Tel. 50 34 37 37
(pp. 108 and 109)

Opened in 1515, this is Bruges' oldest cafe. Its decor, reminiscent of a painting by Van Eyck, provides a gentle transition after a visit to the distant past in the nearby Folklore Museum. Specialties include a large selection of beers and spiked coffees.

SHOPS

CHOCOLATES

It should be noted that all Belgian chocolates, no matter what their supplementary ingredients, are referred to here as "*pralines*." The city is filled with sweet shops run by chocolate-makers themselves. Besides the big names, such as Godiva, Neuhaus and Leonidas, which are sold all over Europe and beyond, here are some smaller ones well worth discovering.

DUMON
Eiermarkt, 6
Tel. 50 34 62 82
Stephane Dumon makes a delicious range chocolates that his mother sells like an angel. Her kindness and courtesy make them indispensable to every customer's well-being.

ALMSHOUSES

There are many almshouses (*Godshuizen*) scattered about the city, each with its visiting hours posted near the entrance. The most interesting are:
the paired complexes of Meulenaere (1613) and St. Joseph (1634) on the corner of Nieuwe Gentweg and Groeninge; Weem (1654), on Drie Korezenstraat; de Vos (1715), at the end of the very narrow Stoofstraat, which leads to Mariastraat; Pelican (1634), at number 8 on the Groenerei; and those attached to the Folklore Museum.

DELDYCKE
Wollestraat, 23
Tel. 50 33 43 35
Among all the *chocolatiers*, there is just one caterer, but what a caterer! This shop carries all the delicacies needed for a perfect picnic in the Bruges countryside, including the essential *filet d'Anvers* (Antwerp filet), dried yet tender slices of beef found only in Flanders. There is also a wide choice of ginevers.

MOEDER BABELUTTE
Marlastraat, 21
Tel. 50 34 75 45
Roszenhoedkaai
Tel. 50 34 56 42
(p. 111)
What this chain of shops lacks in the way of attractive design is made up for in the array of mouthwatering sweets it pureys.

Among the specialties are fruit-filled nougats; hand-made chocolates; and "cuberdons," curious, conical-shaped raspberry confections. "Babelutte" is the name of a particular kind of indigenous caramel.

VAN OOST
Wollestraat, 11
Tel. 50 33 14 54
(p. 111)
This beautiful little shop sells chocolates of exceptional quality.

OTHER SPECIALITIES

TEMMERMAN
Zilverpand
Tel. 50 33 16 78
In the centre of the shopping village of Zilverpand, this attractive store carries an extraordinary range of gingerbread, speculoos, Bruges biscuits and sweet biscuits customarily served with cheese.

DE TROG
Wijngaardstraat, 17
Tel. 50 33 31 37
A pretty blue exterior attracts customers to this excellent bakery, whose offerings include a wide selection of special breads and some twenty-five kinds of croquettes – filled with vegetables, cheese, etc. A vegetarian's delight.

BELGIAN BEER SHOP
Woolstreet company
Wollestraat, 31a
Tel. 50 34 83 83
This shop stocks one of the largest selections of beers to be found anywhere, along with the mugs especially designed for most of the brands.

LACE

LACE

Regrettably, only a handful of shops still sell authentic, hand-made lace, whether antique or of recent vintage.

THE LITTLE LACE SHOP
Markt, 11
Tel. 50 34 54 26
Run by the same family for five generations, this establishment has a large stock of antique lace that it has built up over many years. Some pieces are appliqued on fine linen handerchiefs that themselves have been woven by hand. There are examples of point de rose needlepoint lacework as well as intricate bobbin lace – *point de Paris, rosaine, and rosaline perlee*, with its embroidered raised heart. True marvels.

'T APOSTELIENTJE
Balstraat, 11
Tel. 50 33 78 60
This is a tiny boutique of irresistible charm installed in one of the small houses near the Folklore Museum. The proprietor's husband manufactures lace threads and bobbins that are exported all over the world. The shop stocks old lace and books on the subjet, as well as postcards representing the magnificent

contemporary production of a Bruges-based Japanese lacemaker, Kumiko Nakazaki.

ANTIQUES

KASIMIR'S ANTIQUE STUDIO
Rozenhoedkaai, 3
Tel. 50 34 56 61
This shop near the Groeninge Museum features furniture and *objets* hunted down all over Europe and refurbished to suit contemporary taste.

MEIRE
Sint-Salvadorskerkhof, 9
Tel. 50 33 68 40
Meire is one of Bruges' few bona-fide antique dealers and a connoisseur of the city itself. He specializes in the 17th and 18th century: Flemish furniture, faiences, paintings, Delft ceramic tiles, etc.

POL STANDAERT
Witte Leertouwerstraat, 48
Tel. 50 33 27 32
Stucco workers for several generations, the Standaert family specialize these days in making stucco molds and fireplaces.
The attic where over a century's-worth of the family's production of plasters and molds is stored is open to the public by appointment. One of Bruges' well-kept secrets.

LEATHER GOODS

DELVAUX
Breidelstraat, 2
Tel. 50 49 01 31
Belgium's answer to Hermes. The Bruges outlet at the corner of Markt carries handbags and luggage as well as silk crepe scarves imprinted with the company's exclusive designs.

MUSEUMS

In addition to its two best known museums, the Groeninge (Dijver, 12, tel. 50 44 87 11) and Memling (Mariastraat, 38; same tel.), Bruges has many others that are deserving of attention.

FOLKLORE MUSEUM OF POPULAR ARTS AND TRADITIONS
Rolweg, 40
Tel. 50 33 00 44
(pp. 90, 91)
In the heart of the peaceful St. Anne district, this row of simple houses on a street leading to the Church of Jerusalem is well worth a visit. Its flawless recreations of a Flemish dining room, a pharmacy, a sweet shop, a shoemaker's, a grocery store, a milliners's and a classroom with orderly rows of terraced desks convey vivid impressions of the everyday reality of the past.

GUILD OF THE ARCHERS OF ST. SEBASTIAN
Carmersstraat, 178
Tel. 50 33 16 26
(pp. 92 to 95)
Be sure to check opening hours in order not to miss an opportunity to visit this institution. Audioguides are available.

GRUUTHUSE
Dijver, 17
Tel. 50 44 87 11
(pp. 86, 88 and 89)
It is unfortunate that the faience, copper, silver, tapestries and furniture exhibited in this admirable collection should be accompanied by such sparse commentary, and that what little explanation there is should be comprehensible to Dutch-speakers only.

GUIDO GEZELLE
Rolweg, 64
Tel. 50 44 87 11
The birthplace of the celebrated Flemish poet (1830-1899) is a quiet spot with a romantic garden.

BEGUINE'S HOUSE
Begijnhof De Wijngaard
Wijngaardstraat, 800
Bruges
(pp. 69, 72-73)
See how the Beguines lived. Certain objects capture attention, like the typical cooking pan and the curious closet appointed with a shelf on which a Beguine would take her solitary meals, in accordance with the rules. Retreats of at least three days can be arranged at the beguinage, which is now run by Benedictine nuns, by writing to the Mother Superior.

OUR LADY OF THE POTTERIE
Potterierei, 79
Tel. 50 44 87 78
This former hospital is probably the least visited museum in Bruges, despite the fact that its displays of silver, tapestries and furniture offer rich rewards to anyone who seeks them out.

GUIDED TOURS

GIDSENKRING, ASSOCIATION OF BRUGES GUIDES
't Zweerd, 10
Tel. 50 38 17 64
Jacques van Wijnendaele
Tel. 50 38 05 10
With the verve of amateur scholars, these guides conduct three thematic tours: Illustrious Bruges (from the city hall to the beguinage), Folkloric Bruges (from St. Anne to the guilds), Hanseatic Bruges – Bruges and Europe (from the Genoans' Loge to the Poorters' Loge).

GIDSENBOND, LEAGUE OF GUIDES TO BRUGES AND WEST FLANDERS
Kleine Hertsberge, 3
Tel. 50 33 22 33
These guides offer tours organized around many themes, among them literary Bruges, Bruges and Europe, the Renaissance, almshouses, Bruges and women, etc.

Contemporary architecture

three projects for "Brugge 2002"

Inspite of its loyalty to the traditional canon of Flemish architecture, Bruges could not, in its role of European Cultural Capital, afford to ignore the importance of contemporary creativity in this domain. Three major projects were commissioned and realized for the occasion. The first is a moveable bridge for pedestrians and cyclists at the mouth of the Coupure canal, between Gentpoort and Kruispoort. Designed by Swiss architects Conzett, Bronzini and Gartmann, this beautiful structure is also a prototype: the entire bridge can be raised five meters to allow for the passage of boats. The mechanism that effects this displacement consists of eighteen cables wound around two long steel tubes that straddle the canal. The ensemble is visually sober and well integrated into its site, and it functions like a dream.

Similar "architectonic" concerns were at work in the construction on the Zand of a huge concert hall that doubles as a convention centre. From a list of seven finalists, an international jury chose Ghent-based architects Paul Robbrecht and Hilde Daem as the building designers. The husband-and-wife team opted for what they term a "pastoral" solution, whose spare lines and natural materials would tie in with the rural aspect of this southwest section of Bruges, between the cathedral, whose color inspired the tone of the new building's terracotta tile facing, and the wooded shores of Minnewater. According to the architects, the extreme simplicity of the exterior is counterbalanced inside by the sophisticated means by which natural light is utilized to the fullest possible extent. There have been local grumblings – not entirely unexpected – about the building's large mass and perceived incongruence.

Less controversial, perhaps because it is intended to be temporary, is the diaphanous pavilion designed by Japanese architect Toyo Ito for the Burg Square – the very heart of Bruges. The ultra-light, open structure is a thirty-meter-long expanse of lacey, openwork aluminum that seems to hover over a circular pool. Ito's idea was to create a place from which the magnificent architecture of the Burg could be seen from a new perspective – to provide a resolutely contemporary prism through which the treasures of the past could be viewed. The effect is magical. It would be a good idea to leave this graceful structure permanently in place as a delicate symbol of Bruges' renewed stake in the present – and the future.

THUMBNAIL HISTORY

Origins

862: the first Count of Flanders, Baldwin I (dubbed Iron-Arm) builds a fortress on a natural jetty (*brygghia*) used for landing goods from England.
892: the first ramparts are constructed. Thus protected from raids by the Normans, the city prospers, as do its dynamic merchants.
1134: a severe storm changes the coastline, opening up a channel, the Zwin, between the sea and the outskirts of Bruges.
1150: The Count of Flanders Thierry of Alsace accords the city additional privileges which allow the merchants to make and enforce laws. The Flemish Counts defend Bruges in exchange for shares in the city's commercial transactions.
1180: Damme is declared an independent commune and becomes Bruges' official port of entry, signaling the emergence of the largest transit centre of the Middle Ages.
1214: the French King Philiippe Auguste defeats an Anglo-Flemish front at Bouvines.

Economic capital

1244: Begijnhof De Wijngaard (Beguinage of the Vineyard) founded.
1285-1294: the majority of Flanders' exports, notably wool cloth and tapestries, are shipped from Bruges. Trade flourishes: a covered landing stage is constructed. Commercial syndicates are established, attracting dealers and brokers from all over Europe.
1302: having captured the Count of Flanders and his son, French King Philip the Fair subjugates the province and supports an aristocratic oligarchy. The tensions that arise between the nobility and the working classes culminates in the Bruges Matins, a bloody revolt against French domination.
The Battle of the Golden Spurs sees the unprecedented defeat of a constituted army (in this case, French) by a coalition of urban militias.

Golden Age: the Burgundian Period

1369: Still the sticking point in the Franco-British rivalry, the county of Flanders is awarded to the Dukes of Burgundy as part of a marriage dowry. It becomes their preferred place of residence.
1430: the Order of the Golden Fleece is instituted by the Duke of Burgundy, Philip the Good. He marries Isabella of Portugal in Bruges and celebrates the occasion with lavish festivities. The thriving city attracts scholars and artists of renown, not least among them, Jan Van Eyck.

Decline

1524-1713: the marriage of Mary of Burgundy to the Habsburg emperor Maximilian of Austria paves the way for Spanish rule. Religious strife accompanies Bruges' economic plunge.
1604: choked with silt, the Zwin becomes unnavigable. Bruges loses its role as the most important trading centre in northwestern Europe. Almshouses and hospices are established to help the needy.
1713-1794: Under Austrian rule, Bruges loses its regional preeminence to the dynamic port city of Antwerp.
1794-1814: Occupied by France and untouched by the Industrial Revolution, Bruges continues in its downward economic spiral.
1814: the Congress of Vienna reunites the Low Countries and places them under the anti-French stewardship of the House of Orange.
1830: Bruges is designated as the capital of West Flanders in the newly independent state of Belgium.

Signs of Renewal

1896: King Leopold II orders the construction of a huge commercial port at Zeebrugge, which is inaugurated in 1907.
Slowly emerging from hibernation, Bruges begins the processes of restoring its architectural heritage, dredging its canals and putting up new buildings in the image of the old.
1949: welcoming the prestigious College of Europe within its walls, Bruges affirms its stance of open-minded commitment to the future.
1971: the surrounding communes fuse to form a vast urban agglomerate.
2002: Bruges is chosen as one of the cultural capitals of Europe.

BIBLIOGRAPHY

INVITATION TO THE VOYAGE

The melancholy unreality of a city shrouded in mist and reflected in the water of its canals could only serve as powerful inspiration to Charles Baudelaire, the founder and leading light of the Symbolist movement. While never referring to Bruges explicitly, "Invitation to the Voyage," poem number 127 in his 1857 *The Flowers of Evil*, evokes the city's sovereign beauty in every line.

My child, my sister, dream
How sweet all things would seem
Were we in that kind land to live together,
And there love low and long,
There love and die among
Those scenes that image you, that sumptuous weather.
Drowned sums that glimmer there
Through cloud-dishevelled air
Move me with such a mystery as appears
Within those other skies
Of your treacherous eyes
When I behold them shining through their tears.

There, there is nothing else but grace and measure,
Richness, quietnes, and pleasure.

Furniture that wears
The lustre of the years
Softly would glow withing our glowing chamber,
Flowers of rarest bloom
Proffering their perfume
Mixed with the vague fragrances of amber;
Gold ceilings would there be,
Mirrors deep as the sea,
The walls all in an Eastern splendor hung –
Nothing but should address
The soul's loneliness,
Speaking her sweet and secret native tongue.

There, there is nothing else but grace and measure,
Richness, quietness, and pleasure.

See, sheltered from the swells
There in the still canals
Those drowsy ships that dream of sailing forth;
It is to satisfy your least desire, they ply
Hither through all the waters of the eaarth.

The sun at close of day
Clothes the fields of hay,
Then the canals, at last the town entire
In hyacinth and gold;
Slowly the land is rolled
Sleepward under a sea of gentle fire.

There, there is nothing else but grace and measure,
Richness, quietnes, and pleasure.

(translated by Richard Wilbur)

BRUGES-LA-MORTE

In 1892, Flammarion published the Belgian – but also very Parisian – writer Georges Rodenbach's short masterpiece *Bruges-la-Morte*. The novel's dusky, turn-of-the-century mood and "chagrinned tonality," are perfectly attuned to the book's rather morbid subject: the maniacal and finally murderous passion of an inconsolable widower, Hughes Viane, for the memory of his dead wife. Mallarme, whom Rodenbach (1855-1898) admired, wrote to him when the book came out, "Your human story evaporates, and the city continues as the enlarged ghost ...." Indeed, it is Bruges itself that is the central character of this tale,

or rather, this evocation. For it's a spectral Bruges, far removed from the lively city that we now know.

The photographs that illustrated the first edition served as visual counterpoints to the narrative and underscored this sad vision of a phantom city. With hindsight, they seem to have contributed to nothing less than a singular literary achievement. In their introduction to Flammarion's reedition of that volume in 1998, Pierre Bertrand and Daniel Grojnowski identified it as belonging to a minor but coherent genre: the photo-novel.

Bruges was desperately sad on these late afternoons. But Hughes liked it that way. ...
A mysterious equation was forming: the need for a dead city to correspond to his dead wife. His deep mourning demanded an appropriate setting. Only in Bruges would his life remain bearable. So he had gone there instinctively. Let the world elsewhere bustle, hum, get excited over holidays, braid its thousand yarns. He needed unbroken silence, an existence so monotonous as barely allowing him to feel still alive.

Why must silence prevail in the vicinity of physical suffering? Why do we tread so gently in sickrooms? Why do voices and noises seem to cause disturbances and even reopen wounds? And noise even has a bearing on the suffering of the mind.

In the mute atmosphere of the lifeless waters and streets, Hugues felt his heartache less, and he could think more calmly about his wife. In the line of the canals, he was better able to see and hear her again, to discover her Ophelia face floating along, to listen to her voice in the high-pitched distant song of the carillon.

Equally beautiful and beloved in its former days, the city was the virtual incarnation of Hugues' own loss. Bruges was his wife, while she was Bruges. Their destinies were joined together. This was Bruges-la-Morte, the dead city, entombed in its stone quays, the arteries of it canals chilled to death at the cessation of the great heartbeat of the sea.

INDEX

BIBLIOGRAPHY
Bruges-la-Morte
Georges Rodenbach,
GF Flammarion, 1998
English translation,
Atlas Press, 1993
Bruges la Vive
Dominique Rolin, Ramsay,
1990
Là-bas
Huysmans, GF Flammarion,
1997
The Legend of Ulenspiegel
Charles De Coster,
translation F. M. Atkinson,
London, William
Heinemann Ltd., 1928
The Belfry of Bruges and Other Poems,
Henry Wadsworth
Longfellow, in: *The CompletePoetical Works of Henry Wadsworth Longfellow*,
Buccaneer Books, 1993
Bruges and the Renaissance: Memling to Pourbus,
Maximiliaan P. J. Martens,
ed., exhibition catalogue,
Stichting Kunstboek, 1998;
and New York, Harry N.
Abrams, 1999.
Lace and Costumes, Martine
Bruggeman, Bruges
Municipal Museums, 1995
Hans Memling, The Complete Works, Dirk De Vos, Fonds
Mercator Paribas & Ludion
Press, 1994
Petrus Christus: Renaissance Master of Bruges
Maryan Ainsworth and
Maximiliaan P. J. Martens,
The Metropolitan Museum
of Art, New York, exhibition
catalogue, 1994
Flemish Cities Exlored: Bruges, Ghent, Antwerp, Leuwen, Mechelen & Ostend, Derek
Blyth, Pallas Athene, 3rd
edition, 1998.

The numbers in italics refer to illustrations.

www.lannoo.com

Cover Design:
Studio Lannoo
English translation:
Sarah Mc Phannon
Composition:
Compogravure Guy

Original Publisher:
Editions Flammarion, Paris
D/2002/45/182
ISBN 90 209 4900 4
NUR 520/693

Printed in Italy

PICTURE CREDITS

Page 87, *Madonna with the canon Joris van der Paele*, Stedelijk Museum Bruges, Groeningenmuseum, inv.nr. 0.161.1

ACKNOWLEDGEMENTS

The author is grateful to all those who shared with him their perceptions of Bruges and its secrets – especially Marie-Josee and Carole Bauvin, Lily and Rik Scholiers, Eric Valenjin and Jean-Marc Leblon. He would also like to thank Gisou Bavoillot and Anne-Laure Mojaisky for their valuable assistance in bringing out this book.

The photographer is grateful most particularly to Brigitte Forgeur, Paul Hoste, Marc Nyssen and Francoise Van Den Eynde for their warm welcomes and kind attention.

The editor is indebted to Lily and Rik Scholiers for their generous help and welcoming manner and is most grateful, too, to Ines Sarramon and Bernard Dupre. Special thanks to all those who received us so kindly in Bruges, and in particular to Mr. Hoste and Mrs. Mergaert of the Montanus Hotel, Mrs. Vanhaeke of the Romantik Pandhotel, Mr. Nyssen of De Stamper farm, Mrs. Nuylle of The Little Lace Shop, and Piet Swimberghe.